Preac

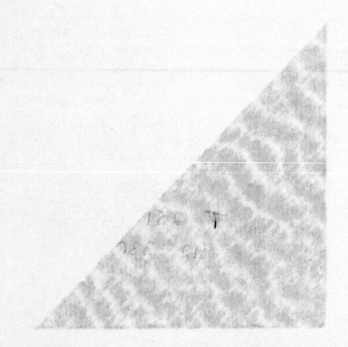

PREACH THE WORD

DENIS LANE

 EVANGELICAL PRESS

EVANGELICAL PRESS
12 Wooler Street, Darlington, Co. Durham, DL1 1RQ, England.
© Evangelical Press 1986

First published 1979
Revised edition 1986
Reprinted 1988

Scripture quotations in this publication are from the Holy Bible,
New International Version. Copyright © 1973, 1978, 1984.
International Bible Society. Published by Hodder and Stoughton.

Lane, Denis
Preach the word. - Rev. ed.
1. Preaching
I. Title
251   BV4211.2

ISBN 0-85234-221-7

Typeset by Inset, Chappel, Essex.
Printed in Great Britain by the Bath Press, Avon.

Contents

Contents

Preface

'Tomorrow is already here and we are all set for yesterday.' I do not know the author of this pithy sentence, but when I first read it the message came through clearly. But is this really what is wrong with the church of God today? That by and large we are ineffective is too plain for argument, but why are we Christians generally so weak? Are we simply out of date? Can we remedy the defect by getting 'with it', or do our problems go much deeper? I believe they do.

Hosea described the problems of his day in terms of lack of knowledge. Ignorance of truth led to ineffectiveness of life. Worse than that, lack of knowledge of God produced a lack of morality as plain as what appears on the pages of any modern newspaper. 'There is no faithfulness, no love, no acknowledgement of God in the land', moaned Hosea, but 'there is only cursing, lying and murder, stealing and adultery . . . because of this the land mourns' (Hos. 4:1,2). Men who have little grasp of truth and little knowledge of God have little hope of stability in their society. Hosea's diagnosis proved true for his day and proves true of ours.

But how many Christians really know what their faith is all about? How many can give a reason for their beliefs? How many see Christian truth as a whole where individual truths fit into the picture?

The prophet carried his diagnosis further and deeper. He did not blame the people but their teachers. 'My people are destroyed from lack of knowledge. Because you have rejected knowledge, I also reject you as priests . . .' (Hos. 4:6,7). The priests who should have been their teachers had rejected knowledge and forgotten the law of their God. Lack of knowledge among the people of God meant a lack of teaching by the servants of God. In Hosea's day the lack of

7

teaching could be traced to refusal to accept the true source of knowledge in God's law. Therefore it is not surprising that today, in churches where men think they know better than to take the Word of God at its face value, there is little understanding of spiritual truth. The real tragedy is, however, that in churches where the Word of God is fully believed and accepted, still the people starve for lack of instruction. Preaching there is in plenty, but little consecutive teaching and not too much result in changed lives. The famine of 'hearing the words of the Lord' described by Amos in 8:11, 12 is only accentuated by the gladness with which the exposition of the Scriptures is welcomed where it can be found.

I speak as a preacher and pastor myself. Why do our people starve in the midst of plenty? I firmly believe that it is because too often we indulge in 'blessed thoughts' and too infrequently teach the Word of God in all its fulness. We take our thoughts and hang them onto Scripture, instead of allowing the Scriptures to control our thoughts. We use a text as a kind of launching platform to be left behind after take-off and we never return to it. Then we say what is from our own hearts and this may have no foundation at all in the text itself. Sincere exhortation and a fund of good stories, however, are no substitute for the convincing power and authority of the Word of God.

Often we do not realize just how little of our preaching is exposition of what the Word of God actually says. We may think we are expounding, when in fact we are not. A simple test will show us whether our preaching and teaching are expository or not. Do our hearers feel compelled to open their Bibles and do they refer to them when we are speaking? Or have they become so accustomed to our 'blessed thoughts' that their Bibles sit closed in front of them, or worse still, lie neglected at home?

What is written above is what I wrote nearly ten years ago in the first edition of this book. Since then, little has occurred to make me feel I should change any of it. The number of those who truly expound the Word of God still seems to be pitifully small. Moreover, in some sections of the church, heavy reliance on direct words from God tends to downgrade the ministry of the Word, sometimes coupled with a false dichotomy between the Spirit of God and the Word of God. I say 'false' because the Spirit is the Author of the Word and any ministry must be tested by that Word.

In the meantime, the decline in the ability of people to concentrate on anything at all for more than a few minutes has reduced the time allowed for preaching even more drastically than before in some Western countries. The whole process is a vicious spiral downwards. Poor preaching invites poor concentration, and poor concentration invites slack preparation. Yet, even today, when the Word of God is expounded in the power of the Spirit of God, people still take notice and ask for more. The challenge, then, is for those who believe that God still honours his Word to commit themselves afresh to excellence in preparation and power in delivery.

Dr James Packer, in his book *Keep in Step with the Spirit*, reminds us that while revival is ultimately the sovereign work of God himself, there are three things for us to do to prepare the way. The first of these is to 'preach and teach, because it is through the truth — Bible truth, gospel truth, truth taken into the mind and heart — that God blesses'.[1] Repentance and prayer must take place too, but the Lord has promised to honour with his blessing the preaching of his Word. I have been encouraged that God has been pleased to use this little book to help some in this ministry, and I pray that this new edition may continue to be used in this way.

1. J. I. Packer, *Keep in Step with the Spirit*, IVP, 1984, p. 257.

1.
Revelation and the Word of God

Modern man finds himself drifting in an ocean of uncertainty and meaninglessness. Barely afloat, he searches the distant line of the horizon in vain. No help is in sight. Everything is relative to everything else. He not only cannot find the truth; he has given up the search. Truth ultimately relates to God, the ultimate reality, and if God is dead or deaf or dumb, truth has no anchor. No wonder then that mankind drifts on to nothingness.

In the midst of this sea of uncertainty the Scriptures still trumpet in Genesis 1:1: 'In the beginning God created . . .' and in John 1:1: 'In the beginning was the Word.' God exists as the ultimate being; we and all creation are made by him and he is a communicating God and has been from the beginning. We do not have to drift. Truth corresponds with what is ultimately real and with an accurate account of reality. Scientific truth corresponds to things as they really are, provided we can respond to them with our physical senses. Religious truth corresponds to God as he is and to life as he meant it to be lived.

We cannot possibly know these things unless God reveals them to us. Indeed we would not know scientific truth if God had not been pleased to give new insights to pioneering professors. Modern man is no more intelligent than his predecessors and is only kidding himself if he thinks he is. He has simply been given some keys that other generations missed.

When we come to meaning in life and ultimate reality, revelation proves absolutely vital. God is personal and relates to man as a person and the means of communication is his Word. John tells us that Jesus Christ, the true Word of God, existed as 'the Word' right in the beginning. When 'the Word became flesh' (John 1:14) God spoke to man and revealed himself to man in a language all could understand, the language of human life. If that truly happened, as we Christians believe, then we have a source for understanding God, man, life, death and all of importance that concerns them.

The only means by which we can possibly know this Word of God is through the written Word that his immediate followers penned in the power of the Spirit. His life lies before us in the Gospels; his risen activity through the Spirit flows through Acts. The epistles enlarge our understanding of his being and apply his teaching and power to human situations and Revelation puts him into the context of eternal history. We discover also that the Old Testament, with all its imagery and prophecy, points forward to this one living, definitive Word of God.

When, therefore, we underline the importance of the written Word of God, we are not worshipping or idolizing a book, but seeing beyond the book to the God who has been communicating to man through the words of that book, its acts and explanations, from the beginning of time. We have no other reliable source. Every other expression of opinion on reality is a guess.

John 1:18 puts things very clearly: 'No one has ever seen God,' so no human description of him can be relied upon. 'But God the only Son, who is at the Father's side, has made him known.' Only one person has any claim to accuracy and that claim rests on a unique relationship and a present position. As the only Son, Jesus Christ possesses a unique knowledge of God and, being at his Father's side, he is in a peculiar position to reveal God accurately. This one person has 'made him known'.

In saying that, John uses a Greek word of great interest to any preacher. From it, we receive our word 'exegesis', meaning to 'lead out from'. In other words, Jesus, from his relationship and position, was the only one who could and did take the truth that lay hidden in the innermost heart and being of God and bring it out into the light of day for us to see and understand.

In doing this, even Jesus Christ himself possessed no freedom to diverge from the truth within God. He simply had to 'lead such truth out' for all to see. He was faithful in this to the end. The role of the preacher is exactly the same. Our task, however, is harder. We have no unique relationship to God such as Jesus had, except through our relationship to him. We have to strive much harder to find the truth of God and to make it plain for all to see. We are bound, as he was bound, to keep within the borders of accurate expression of what is really there in God's being and heart. He could rely on the directness of his unique relationship and position. We must seek the truth in Jesus Christ, the living Word, and we can only find that truth through the written Word. So we are twice removed from his position.

Yet we are not left entirely without help. Far from it! Before he left this world Jesus himself promised 'another Counsellor to be with you for ever — the Spirit of truth' (John 14:16, 17). Paul in turn pointed out, 'We have not received the spirit of the world but the Spirit who is from God, that we may understand what God has freely given us.' Moreover he went on to claim, 'This is what we speak, not in words taught us by human wisdom but in words taught by the Spirit, expressing spiritual truths in spiritual words' (1 Cor. 2:12, 13). Though we are subject to limitations Jesus did not have and removed from his times by two thousand years, the Spirit of God is still with us to enable us both to understand and to explain God's truth to men and women.

If modern man is to be saved from shipwreck in his sea of uncertainty he has therefore to be called back to the whole concept of truth. Truth does exist and can be found. Jesus Christ took all the truth of God and faithfully expressed things as they really are. He told it like it is. But modern man can only be brought back if we in our generation will be faithful to the truth as it is in Jesus Christ. That means confining ourselves to the testimony to him that we find in the Scriptures and seeking the aid of his Spirit for our understanding and the power of his Spirit in communication. In other words, we must return to preaching the Word of God in the power of the Spirit. We must come back to that Word, in full trust that here is where we find truth revealed and expressed. We must stop ignoring

this Word and become its servants. We must stop sitting in
judgement upon it and start letting it sit in judgement upon
us. Such preaching is, I believe, the essence of biblical
prophecy, telling forth and applying to a contemporary
generation the truths of God and his Word. As Dr J. I. Packer
expresses it in his excellent book *Keep in Step with the
Spirit*, 'Prophecy has been and remains a reality whenever
and wherever Bible truth is genuinely *preached* — that is,
spelled out and applied, whether from a pulpit or more
informally. Preaching is teaching God's revealed truth with
application; such teaching with application is prophecy,
always was and always will be . . .'[1] Our generation des-
perately needs such prophecy and such prophets.

1. J. I. Packer, *Keep in Step with the Spirit*, IVP, 1984, p. 217.

2.
The preacher and his message

Truth through personality

The church of God across the world needs men of God in the ministry. Where such men are lacking some people are not listening to the command of God, and what applies to churches also applies in mission.

God has chosen to pass his message through people. His supreme revelation of himself came to us in a man, the Word made flesh. In Jesus Christ truth had a perfect human medium through which to reach us. The rays of true light were not bent, darkened or hindered by passing through the transparent personality of the Lord.

Despite our failings, God still chooses to bring truth to men through other men. Philip Brooks, in his famous *Lectures on Preaching,* describes preaching as 'truth mediated through personality'. 'God,' says Paul in 2 Corinthians 5:20, is 'making his appeal through us' in our position as ambassadors for Christ. Effective preaching depends on much more than good speaking, careful construction of the message and knowledge of methods. What we *are* determines the kind of message our hearers receive. Our personality and personal relationship with God are vital parts of our preaching. We cannot live carelessly from Monday to Saturday and expect to preach with power on Sunday.

Jeremiah's call and ministry underline the importance God attaches to the person of the speaker. God knew him before he was born, consecrated and appointed him a prophet before Jeremiah himself could walk around the room (Jer. 1:5). He had no choice about his work and his objections on account of his age were brushed aside by the command to go to the people God wanted to speak to,

15

with the message they needed to hear (Jer. 1:7). Jeremiah
was to speak, and the result would be God's words in his
human mouth, truth mediated through personality (Jer.
1:9). The authority thereby given to Jeremiah's position
is repeated again and again in Scripture with men like Moses,
Samuel, Elijah, Isaiah and Daniel. God's ways do not change.
God's method is still men.

What greater privilege, then, can any of us have than to
be called of God to be his messenger to our own people
today? Yet how few are happy to accept this calling for
themselves or their children, if the door to medicine or law
or some other well-paid profession remains open!

God's plan

Let us look more closely at the preacher and his own position
in God's plan for bringing truth to men. John the Baptist
pointed his generation towards Christ. His ministry is
described in Mark 1:2: 'I will send my messenger ahead of
you, who will prepare your way.'

1. His command
Firstly, the only justification for preaching is the God-given
confidence that God has said, 'I am sending you' (cf. Ezek.
2:3,4). This command cannot be refused. When God sends
we must obey, whatever our plans, however good our
education, whatever our family thinks. If God does not send,
we dare not go. When God sends we must go (1 Cor. 9:16,
17). The church needs men of God in the ministry. Why
then are so few coming forward, especially from the ranks
of university graduates? Does God not call, or are some
people not listening?

2. His messenger
Secondly, John the Baptist is described as 'my messenger'
and in these two words lie both the glory and the humility
of the preacher. To be the messenger of the living God, the
Creator of the universe, is as high a privilege as can ever be
given to a man. Yet at the same time to be a messenger is
to be given a humble position of responsibility. A messenger

is a nobody, sent by somebody with a communication. His responsibility rests in passing on the message. He is not important, and his only privilege lies in the person who sent him. The messenger does not construct the message; he only delivers it. He must not change it or give it his own meaning. He is the servant not only of the one who sent him, but also of the message with which he is sent.

3. His forerunner

Thirdly, in the case of the preacher, the messenger has the particular responsibility of 'preparing your way' or 'preparing the way for the Lord'. He goes in front to prepare his hearers for someone vastly more important who himself intends to come. The preacher's job consists of delivering the message and then getting out of the way. 'He must become greater; I must become less' could well be set over every place where men preach. Sometimes I feel like crying out to the preacher in the middle of his message, 'Get out of the way, man, get out of the way.' He comes across well, but his Lord remains hidden in the messenger's shadow.

The same combination of privilege and responsibility, of glory and humility appears again and again in Scripture. A particularly clear passage is 2 Corinthians 5:20 which may be set out as in Table I.

Table I. Analysis of 2 Corinthians 5:20

We are therefore Christ's ambassadors	Representing the God who called us.
as though God were making his appeal	With his divine authority.
through us —	Through the human personality.
we implore you	Through the human personality.
on Christ's behalf;	With his authority.
Be reconciled to God.	The message we are to convey.

As we have seen, the preacher clearly occupies a place of particular privilege and special responsibility. He has a high office to occupy and a humble service to give. What, then, should be the marks of those of us called to be preachers of the Word of God? We will look at these marks in relation to God, to the message and to the hearers.

Marks of an expository preacher

1. A sense of the greatness and reality of God

Unless we *feel* with our hearts as well as *know* with our minds the reality and greatness of the living God, our message will carry no conviction. Isaiah needed to see the Lord high and exalted, reigning, worshipped, his glory filling the earth, before he could begin his ministry (Isa. 6:1–8). Ezekiel saw God, hidden yet self-revealing, always moving yet never changing, self-consistent, reigning over all, holy yet merciful (Ezek. 1). Daniel's strength drained from him as he fell on his face before the reality that is God (Dan. 10:2–9). John the apostle fell at the feet of the risen Christ like a dead man when the vision burst upon him (Rev. 1:12–17). Even the Lord himself spent forty days and nights alone submitting himself to his Father's will before beginning his ministry. 'Listen to men who listen to God,' A. W. Tozer advised Christians. Part of our poverty in preaching today is poverty in our knowledge of God.

2. A sense of helplessness apart from God's enabling

Isaiah saw the Lord himself dealing with the problem of his unclean lips. Ezekiel was told to stand on his feet and was given the Spirit to enable him to do so. The Lord put his hand on Daniel and set him at first on trembling hands and knees and then in a fully upright position. John was told not to fear, as the Lord's right hand touched his prostrate body. The man who has known the greatness and reality of God does not speak lightly or quickly. He knows in truth as well as in theory that without Christ we can do nothing (John 15:5). The world chatters on today, but few men speak from the presence of God in a conscious dependence on his power. Our world is full of words but

knows little of the Word that comes from God. We cannot
bring others that Word without taking the time to listen to
what God has to say to us first.

3. *Responsibility to make the message a part of himself*

When Ezekiel was commissioned to preach he was told to
open his mouth and to eat what God gave him (Ezek. 2:8).
He then saw the message written out before him on a scroll,
and it was anything but pleasant. The scroll was filled with
'words of lament and mourning and woe', and no man is
anxious to proclaim such a message. He was warned, however, to eat the scroll, to 'fill his stomach with it' and to 'go'.
When he obeyed, the taste of the Word of God, despite its
unpleasant message, was sweet as honey to his mouth.
Clearly, as a preacher he was to receive it into his own
heart, to hear it with his own ears and to make it thoroughly
a part of himself before he went to speak to other people.
In the same way, the apostle John in his First Epistle (1 John
1:1–3) commended the truth to men. This truth was 'the
word of life'. He could commend this Word because he had
heard, seen, looked upon and touched it for himself. The
message came from his heart and personal experience. Likewise in Isaiah 50:4, 5 the prophet had 'an instructed tongue'
and he knew 'the word that sustains the weary'. What
preacher would not covet such an ability in his ministry?
Isaiah gained that ability because morning by morning God
had wakened him to listen like one being taught, and he
had been ready to respond despite the suffering and shame
involved (vv. 5, 6). As George Adam Smith says, 'The prophet
learns his speech as the little child by listening. Grace is
poured upon the lips through the open ear.' Significantly
this passage is a prophecy of Christ himself. The morning-
by-morning listening of the preacher to the voice of God
should be a fruitful source of material for ministry to others,
but it is a demanding task.

I have been surprised in my travels to find how many
Christian ministers fail to have that regular time in the day
which Christians of my generation called the 'quiet time'.
I have found over thirty years of preaching that this time
early in the morning is for me not only the most precious
time of the day, but the wellspring of my messages. Many

times I have been asked what I do during this period, so, at
the risk of stating what to some may be obvious, I will set
it down here.

I use the early morning, because that is the time when
I am really alert and, living as I do most of the time 3°
north of the equator, it is the coolest and most beautiful
time of day. I do not function after 10 p.m., but my friend
who only begins to get going then, and for whom the early
mornings are the sleepy time, has his special time often at
midnight. We are all different and we need to know ourselves.

I begin by reading something mentally stimulating and
often doctrinal. This puts my mind into gear and turns my
thoughts towards God. Then I pray for the Spirit's leading
and turn to the Scriptures, taking a book at a time. For
twenty minutes to half an hour I will study that particular
Bible book, making notes on loose-leaf paper for subsequent
filing in ring binders. On these sheets I record the fruit of
study and meditation on the next few verses. These may be
one or two or twenty or thirty, depending on the kind of
passage. Sometimes I will use a commentary to supplement
my own study, going through the whole book with the one
commentary over a period of time. By this means I finish
up with a ring binder on a Bible book that contains notes
of things I have found spiritually valuable, challenging or
stimulating. Although I do not study with preaching in
mind, these notes form an invaluable storehouse for future
messages, a storehouse I can never exhaust. This also means
that when I come to preach on a passage, the Lord has
already used it to my heart first. The truth has gone through
my personality.

The rest of that morning watch I use for prayer, beginning
with the truths assimilated that morning, moving into
worship and then into intercession for family, friends, fellow
workers and the wider world.

4. Courage to express what he has received from God
Jeremiah was warned not to decry his youthfulness (Jer. 1:
6—8), nor to be dismayed by reactions to his preaching
(Jer. 1:17—19). His hearers would fight against him, but his
God would make him a fortified city and would be there to
deliver him.

Ezekiel was told that if he had gone to a people of a foreign language they would have listened to him, but his own people were hard-headed and stubborn-hearted. God promised to harden Ezekiel's head more than theirs, though he never spoke of hardening his heart (Ezek. 3:5—11).

The youthful Samuel was warned by the aged Eli not to keep to himself a message God had given him for others (1 Sam. 3:17,18).

Courage can be confused with bigotry and needs tempering with humility and genuine concern, but is an essential requirement for a preacher.

5. Willingness to learn and obey God's Word

In relation to his hearers the preacher must sit under the Word of God with them. His position in the pulpit does not place him above the Word because God may have as much to say to him as to his hearers. Paul told Timothy to 'command and teach these things' in 1 Timothy 4:11. 'These things' were actually commands already given to Timothy himself in the preceding verses. He was to be nourished in the truths of the faith and of the good teaching which he followed. He was to have nothing to do with godless myths and old wives' tales, and so on.

6. Concern to understand and meet the hearers' needs

Some preachers rarely visit their congregations. How can they understand people whom they do not know? The Word of God does not change from generation to generation, but it does need to be freshly applied to the hearts and minds of men in terms which they can understand. Ezekiel had to go and sit among the exiles himself before he could begin his ministry (Ezek. 3:15) and he found it an overwhelming experience. Moses endured forty years of the wilderness before God called him to lead the people of Israel through the same blistering desert. The Lord himself was able to preach to publicans and sinners because he thoroughly understood them. How essential therefore for the preacher to have regular up-to-date contact with the people to whom he ministers, in their thoughts, hopes, fears and desires! He is not to accommodate the gospel to them to make it more popular, but he must be able to apply the gospel to

their needs in terms that are relevant to them. Jesus' illustrations were drawn from everyday life. They spoke to the
heart.

I have spent considerable space on the place of the
preacher for this is the key to effective preaching. The Lord
Jesus Christ had the most effective ministry of all because,
on the one hand, he was in the closest living contact with
his Father, and on the other, he was in continuous vital
contact with ordinary men. When he spoke, he spoke in
the name and from the presence of the living God. He also
spoke to the needs of the men of his own day so that they
went away with lasting impressions of the authority of his
teaching (Mark 1:22) and the depth of his understanding. If
we would be effective preachers and teachers of the Word
we must listen to God and understand men. For the preacher
this involves the tension between the study and the street,
between pulpit preaching and pastoral visiting. Both are
essential to a truly effective ministry.

Study questions

1. Make a study of one or all of the following passages:
   Isaiah 6; Jeremiah 1; Ezekiel 1–3:27; Daniel 10;
   Revelation 1:9–20.
   Note down especially:
   a. how the person saw and experienced God;
   b. the relation between his particular vision and the
       needs of the people of his day;
   c. how the preacher felt about himself;
   d. how God made the preacher feel able to do his work;
   e. the qualities required of the preacher;
   f. the content and limitations of his message.
2. How did each of these preachers identify with their
   people?
3. What things in the personal lives and histories of these
   preachers did God use to fit them for their ministry?
4. How can we develop our knowledge and vision of God?

3.
The nature of expository preaching

When we speak of expository preaching, what do we really mean? Most preaching begins with a biblical text, so there is obviously more to it than that.

Old Testament background

The best way to understand true exposition is to look at the nature of preaching in the Scriptures. An example is in the book of Nehemiah 8:1—8.

1. Eager listeners
The first thing we notice here is the background to the preaching. Verse 1 speaks of all the people gathering as one man in the square before the Water Gate and of their telling Ezra the scribe to bring the Book of the Law of Moses 'which the Lord had commanded for Israel'. Here was a people united in their desire to hear the Word of God and recognizing the Book of the Law of Moses not simply as the writing of one of their patriarchs but as the gift of God to his people. They wanted to hear what God had to say to them. They were an extremely eager congregation, for Ezra read from the book from early morning until midday and they were all ears to hear him. Happy is the preacher who has a congregation hungry for the Word of God, as opposed to the man whose elders or deacons or council make it clear that ten minutes is all that they can stand!

2. Submission
The gathering was not held in the temple or any other special building, but Ezra the scribe stood on a wooden

pulpit so that when he spoke to them 'he was standing above' all the people. When he opened the book the people stood up and the impression given is that they stood for the whole of the discourse. Many people object today to the symbolism of the pulpit above the congregation, forgetting that the symbol is not that of the preacher's infallibility but of the people's submission to the Word of God. There was also strong unity on this occasion and Ezra's fellow leaders stood with him, thereby emphasizing their united acceptance of the authority of the Law.

3. Worship

Before Ezra began to expound the Word of God he 'praised the Lord, the great God; and all the people lifted their heads and responded, "Amen! Amen!" Then they bowed down and worshipped the Lord with their faces to the ground' (v. 6). While there is no reason why the ministry of the Word of God has to take place at the same time in the service each week, there is good scriptural reason for preparing the heart to receive the Word through worship. As any preacher knows, the quality of the worship in the church makes his task easier or harder.

A definition

So much for the background. What we are mainly interested in is the example of good exposition that verse 8 clearly describes for us. Really it is quite simple. First of all they read from the book, which all of them recognized as the Law of God. In modern times we not only hear the Word read, but can read and follow for ourselves in our own Bibles. They did not have copies of their own. 'They read from the Book of the Law of God, *making it clear* and *giving the meaning* so that the *people could understand* what was being read.' There was more to this than making the people understand the actual words that were being read. They needed to understand the sense, that is, they needed to know what that particular part of the Word of God had to say to them in their day and in their circumstances. Only then could the people take the Word away with them and put it into practice.

Exposition of the Scripture, therefore, is that process whereby the meaning of a particular passage in the Bible is so explained in terms of the needs and circumstances of the congregation that the people understand what God is saying to them. An essential part of exposition must then be to draw a parallel between the circumstances when the passage was written and the circumstances existing today, so that the principles of the Word of God that never change can be interpreted in the light of present needs. In Ezra's day, not only did the people understand the reading, but the exposition was soon translated into action. Preaching that does not cause that to happen is of little value.

The preaching had an emotional result and in verse 9 the people began to weep. The hearts of the people were stirred. We must not be afraid to move people deeply.

In verses 10–12 the immediate result was that 'All the people went away to eat and drink, to send portions of food and *to celebrate with great joy* because *they now understood* the words that had been made known to them' (v. 12). Nothing should be more joyful than a heart understanding of the grace and goodness of God towards his people. If only more messages preached led to spontaneous giving, rejoicing and feasting!

The ministry that day finally resulted in the people implementing the command to hold the Feast of Tabernacles, 'and their joy was very great' (vv. 13–17).

True biblical exposition is not meant just to interest the minds of men, but to influence their wills to action. The process involves informing the mind, but also moving the heart and stirring the will.

New Testament examples

We now turn to some examples of exposition in the New Testament. They are not in the strict context of preaching, but none the less show clearly the basic principles of exposition.

1. The master translator
Both come in Luke 24 and both come from the Lord Jesus

Christ himself. On the road to Emmaus we read, 'Beginning with Moses and all the Prophets, he explained to them what was said in all the Scriptures concerning himself' (v. 27). He explained the Scriptures for them and Luke uses a word for explanation which in Acts 9:36 is expressed as 'translate'. Translation is the process by which language not immediately understood by the hearer is made understandable. We are familiar with this in ordinary life. The process of exposition does just this for the Scriptures. The job of the preacher is to take language which may be hard to understand because of lack of knowledge of background circumstances, history or other reasons and to give the language meaning in terms that everyone can understand.

2. The master expositor

You will notice also that Jesus began with Moses and the prophets. He used the Old Testament. That was all he had, but it was enough. The two on the road to Emmaus could not understand how it was that Christ should suffer and die. Jesus took the Old Testament and showed them from place after place how God had said that it would happen that way. We often find the Old Testament difficult. In fact, if we are honest, most of us rarely preach from it. The customs and culture and history of Israel seem so far removed from twentieth-century life. Yet basically man has not changed. He still loves and fears, hates and hopes as he did in those days of Scripture. What is needed is for someone to translate the lasting principles of action into terms that relate to the life of modern man. That is the job of the preacher. Just as the Lord Jesus could take the whole sweep of the Old Testament and show them 'what was said . . . concerning himself', so we should be able to see Christ there and explain him to our hearers. Jesus' message that day was a Scripture-based, Christ-centred explanation that left their hearts burning within them. True exposition does just that.

In verse 44 of the same chapter we have another illustration of exposition. This time the text was taken from the Lord's own words: 'This is what I told you while I was still with you.' He then went on to show that these words which he had spoken were in accordance with the words written about him in the Law, the Prophets and the Psalms;

in other words, in all three major divisions of the Hebrew Scriptures. In verses 45–47 the Lord then 'opened their minds so they could understand the Scriptures'; this was exposition. The word for 'opening their minds' is one that means to open completely or thoroughly, and is used elsewhere of opening the eyes of the blind, of Stephen's seeing heaven opened (Acts 7:56), of the Lord's opening Lydia's heart (Acts 16:14) and again of Jesus' opening the Scriptures to them in Luke 24:32.

An expositor's role

The expositor should be able to take the Word of God and to open men's eyes to the application of that Word to every-day life. He is a servant of that Word and of the people. He is not there to impress the people with his fund of good stories or his cleverness in declaring his own views. He is to find what God has said and is still saying through the Scriptures and to apply that in the power of the Spirit to the hearts of the people and to his own heart.

The expositor is in fact dealing with three different 'worlds'. He has to understand the world of the Bible and the historical, cultural and spiritual situations associated with that world. He has to know the present world in which his people live, in order that his message may 'scratch where it itches' and be clearly relevant to the current situation, culture and needs of the people. He must also know his own world and be able to disentangle himself from some aspects of that world that is often so far removed from that of his people. Let me illustrate my meaning.

The Bible world is like a slide transparency, miniature in size, hard to see and sometimes dark to the eye. In fact the slide itself may be crystal clear, very interesting and perfectly taken, but on its own it conveys little meaning to the casual observer and could easily be thrown away as useless. What that slide needs is a projector to focus it clearly, light to illuminate the picture and enlargement to make it plain.

The preacher plays the role of the projector. Aided by the light of the Spirit, his task is to enlarge, make plain and bring into focus what previously was dark and difficult to understand. The projector is not meant to change the slide, but to illuminate it. Of course, if the projector itself is out of focus or the lens is dirty, it is no wonder if people dismiss the slide as useless. The image from the slide passes through the lens just as truth passes through the preacher's personality. This is the point at which the preacher must understand his own world and be able to think himself out of it. In most cases that world is highly academic, strongly theological and largely ecclesiastical. If the message is too strongly dominated by such approaches, the final picture is liable to be very fuzzy to the average person.

I am not suggesting an anti-intellect, anti-theology approach. We must use our minds. A passage of Scripture must be seen in the light of a theology. My concern is that unless we can appreciate how different the preacher's way of approach is from that of the average congregation, we will be talking over people's heads. We will use concepts and terms that carry no more power than a foreign language. Because many preachers fail to discipline themselves to think outside their own world, preaching fails to move people.

A slide also needs a screen on which the enlarged image can be thrown. At that point the light becomes focused, the miniature becomes clearly seeable, the dark becomes light and the mysterious becomes plain. The congregation is the screen, on whose lives the biblical truth must be focused so that the truth becomes translated into action. Unless the preacher understands where his people are and what their needs and problems are, he will fail in this last vital step. Indeed each step is vital to the whole communication process.

Exposition may sound quite simple from the above description, but the sad fact is that few preachers engage in it. Our messages then carry little of the authority of God and his Word behind them and while they may move our people temporarily, do not build them up in their faith or send them back to their Bibles to find out if these things are really so. Again, we may test ourselves by asking how many of our listeners even bring their Bibles with them and, when they do, how often they feel compelled to refer to them.

Study questions

Study Peter's sermon on the Day of Pentecost (Acts 2: 14–41).

1. What passage of Scripture did Peter use as a basis?
2. How was this explained in terms of the needs and circumstances of his hearers?
3. What evidence do you find that Peter made men think? Trace the development of his argument. What was the climax?
4. How do you know Peter moved the *hearts* of the people? What particular words of his sermon were especially aimed to do this?
5. What did Peter expect the people to *do* as a result of his message?
6. How many deep theological ideas did Peter bring into his sermon? How were they relevant?

4.
Planned preaching

Aim at nothing and you are sure to hit it. To preach on a different subject each week with no overall Spirit-guided plan in mind is to develop a congregation who have little overall grasp of the faith. Christian truth is a consistent whole. We are told to have our loins girded with the truth. The Roman soldier's armour held together because of the belt around his loins, and the Christian's armour holds together by an overall grasp of the truth as a body of teaching. How can we expect our people to have such a grasp of truth if they listen to a different preacher each week? To give the pulpit ministry to a visitor may be a sign of humility in a pastor but asks for spiritual weakness in a congregation. How also can they have an overall grasp of the truth if every Sunday's sermon is quite unrelated to what went before and what comes after? Regrettably, some Christians' spiritual diet consists only of the sermons they hear on Sunday. What kind of food do we plan for them?

I am convinced that regular expository preaching carefully planned ahead is the best way to feed a congregation. Let me give several reasons why.

Reasons for planned expository preaching

1. By preaching to a plan, whether it be by going through a book or by covering certain subjects, the whole of God's plan can be unfolded

We are delivered from being bound to our own pet themes. Next Sunday we have to go on with the letter to the Romans, or whatever it is, and we preach on what the next passage says, not on what we would like it to say. Have you ever sat under a preacher who has a pet theme? The theme may be the ABC of the gospel, a very good theme, but even that wears thin when he finds it in every single passage and preaches on little else. The congregation, too, get to know what is coming and their minds turn off at the start.

2. Regular exposition enables us to deal with some important matters of Christian living in a natural way

The life of Joseph contains the temptation to sexual sin with Potiphar's wife. He would be a bold pastor who suddenly and with no apparent reason chose that passage for a sermon. People would ask themselves what or whom he was getting at, or whether he himself had some strange kink in his make-up. But this kind of subject needs dealing with today. So many Christians never receive teaching to prepare them for marriage or to enable them to face a world without moral standards. A series of messages on Joseph's life would make it quite natural to speak on sexual temptation without anyone asking why.

3. As the congregation begin to hear planned expository preaching, they start to think ahead

They want to know what is going to happen next. They may even be interested enough to look up a passage before they come. While they are listening in church they will be encouraged to refer to the passage to understand its meaning, and therefore they are more likely to bring their Bibles along. They are beginning to need them. Furthermore, careful, simple exposition may set them studying for themselves, and a spiritual, ethical, time bomb will have been planted in their lives that will eventually explode with untold benefit to the church.

4. Ethics, both personal and social, will begin to take their place in the regular teaching

Most evangelical preaching is doctrinal. Doctrine is especially vital today, with so many theologies without content drifting around. The epistles are full of doctrine, but they are also full of ethics. How often are these ethical standards brought before people today? When did you last hear or preach a sermon on employer/employee, husband/wife or parent/child

relationships? Dishonesty in business causes untold agony
for Christians today. Do they know what the Bible says
about this and how the early Christians worked it out in
their day?

5. The Old Testament will have its place in planned expository preaching

How often does that happen in your local church? Yet how
up-to-date is Amos with his thundering denunciation of social
injustice and oppression! How contemporary are God's
judgements on unjust societies in Isaiah and Jeremiah! How
relevant to the questions we ask are those that Habakkuk
asked God! The gospel is not primarily a social programme.
Yet the gospel does have social implications and sometimes,
because we do not teach them, thinking, caring people
dismiss the church as irrelevant. Haggai and Zechariah faced
the problems of a developing society striving to get on its
feet after seventy years of chaos and neglect and with a
people depressed and despondent. The whole counsel of
God includes all these issues.

Expository preaching, however, is like dieting. You do
not notice any difference for a time, but over a longer
period imperceptibly the figure changes and the benefits
become apparent. In an age of instant this and that we
expect immediate results. Sometimes God graciously gives
them, but Jesus himself spoke a parable of the kingdom of
God in which he warned that the seed needs time to grow
and often matures out of the sight of men (Mark 4:26–29).

Paul in Romans 12:2 challenged believers to be 'trans-
formed by the renewing of your mind', a continuous gradual
process. I like to compare it to a path through long grass.
The first time you walk through the grass you make little
impact, but if you keep following that path again and again
it gradually becomes easier to follow. Biblical truth passing
through the mind once may make little impact, but constant
re-emphasis through regular biblical exposition eventually
wears a transforming path that effectively changes conduct.

Factors to consider in planned expository preaching

1. We must be careful first of all to ensure an adequate balance in our preaching

All ethics would be as bad as none at all. Some preachers have been able to go straight through a book like the letter to the Romans expounding just a verse or part of a verse each week and still maintain interest. Few of us can do this. By all means let us teach through Romans, but most of us will need to cover more than one verse in a week and to break off from the series every now and then to deal with something quite different. Variety is essential in any diet.

2. We should aim to cover the foundation truths of the faith at least once a year

Whether our denomination agrees or disagrees with 'the church's year' we should regularly cover the doctrines of the birth, death, resurrection and ascension of the Lord and his gift of the Spirit. Without regular reminders, Jesus' second coming and similar truths gradually cease to affect our thinking and our living. Forward thinking through a year enables us to cover what is needed.

3. In preserving a balance in our preaching we need to be very firm with ourselves about our pet themes

Having sat under a ministry that came back again and again each week to the same point, and having heard and seen the reaction of the congregation, I know how easily we can deceive ourselves. A good wife, or a faithful deacon or elder whom we trust, can help keep a check on us here.

4. We must also reckon on the spiritual, emotional and intellectual needs of our congregation

The Corinthians could take only 'milk', but the Romans were obviously able to digest much more solid meat. To feed meat to babies leads to indigestion. To feed milk to mature adults will make them look elsewhere for food. They do not find what they need when they come. Nor must we confuse the grasp of spiritual truth with intellectual brightness. Some very clever people need 'milk' in spiritual matters and some very simple people by the guidance of the Spirit can rejoice in strong 'meat'.

*5. We must be careful to preach within a theological frame-
   work*

This may seem to contradict what was said in the previous
chapter. What I mean is that the whole body of theology is
like a completed jigsaw puzzle and individual truths are like
the pieces. We do not necessarily have to call attention to
the whole picture every time we put in a piece, but as those
trained to see the whole picture we at least must be aware
where the pieces fit together. Otherwise the picture given
will be very lopsided.

Suggested expository series

Let me suggest some series of expositions. You may, for
instance, take a self-contained section of the Word of God.
The Lord's prayer is a good example. By taking each clause
of that prayer in successive weeks you will cover the following truths:

The fatherhood of God   — our Father
The transcendence of God   — in heaven
The holiness of God   — hallowed be your name
The rule of God   — your kingdom come
The purpose of God   — your will be done

These last three messages would all be governed by the clause
'on earth as it is in heaven'. God's majesty, rule and purpose
must all be as fully acknowledged in true Christian living on
earth as they undoubtedly govern all behaviour in heaven.

Having acknowledged the vertical dimension of life, the
second half of the series will deal with relationship to our
needs and to other people. The subjects dealt with will be:

Material need and provision   — Give us today our daily bread
Spiritual need of forgiveness — Forgive us our debts as we
                                also have forgiven our
                                debtors
Spiritual need of protection — And lead us not into temp-
                                tation, but deliver us from
                                the evil one.

You will have covered the two great commandments of love to God and love to your neighbour and will have pointed people to all the ingredients of healthy Christian living. You will also have covered subjects like:

the place of prayer in Christian living;
prayer as submission and worship, not just asking for things;
the relative importance of material and spiritual matters in a materialistic age.

When you have finished, your people should know more of the nature of God, the place of prayer and the right use of material possessions, and should be in a much better position to understand what it means to live as man should live, as a creature before his Creator.

Suggested expository subjects

1. A Bible book

You may decide to preach through a book. Jonah, for example, shows the reluctant missionary, racially prejudiced and determined at all costs to avoid God's pursuing love. The four chapters divide his story very effectively and even though a congregation may have few reluctant missionaries, there are usually several people running away from God, refusing his love, grumbling at his dealings with them or forgetting God's love for those of other nations and races. Jonah is right up-to-date.

2. The life of a Bible character

The life of a Bible character provides living illustrations of God's dealings with men. Their environment was different and the amount of knowledge they had to go on was much less, but they feared and hoped, schemed and planned, loved and hated, cheated and even murdered just as man still does.

3. A chapter of the Bible

This might be something like John 19 or Mark 14, tracing the last days and hours of Christ. In Mark 14 you have tremendous pictures of human nature in relation to Jesus Christ in the following:

The great devotion of the woman (vv. 1–11).
The great betrayal of Judas (vv. 12–21, 43–45).
The great desertion of the disciples (vv. 27–51).
The great denial of Peter (vv. 27–31, 53, 54, 66–72).

4. A theme such as prayer, or the signs of Jesus' coming, or the work of the Holy Spirit
Whatever you do needs regular realistic assessment, continued planning and careful thought as to how long each series should be. Some people may fear the limiting of the Spirit of God in all this. There is no real basis for this fear. The Spirit can guide you six months ahead as easily as six hours or six minutes. If he tells you to scrap the subject for the day you can do it. He normally works through the minds of men in an orderly fashion. Planning can be as prayerful as last-minute preparation.

Study questions

1. Draw up headings for a series of sermons on John 19, the life of Jacob and 1 Thessalonians.
2. Write down when you last preached (or heard someone else preach) on marriage (not a wedding), Christian business methods, prayer, the second coming of Christ and the meaning of repentance. What passages would you expound to teach these truths?
3. If you had (or have) the freedom to decide on a series of messages in your church to last six Sundays and you wanted to meet the most important spiritual needs of your congregation, what would you preach on, which Bible passages would you use and under what headings would you announce your six subjects?

5.
The preparation - basic outlines

Now we move on to the practical details of preparing to
expound the Scriptures. I am conscious that what I say from
now on is very much how God has led me. I have a tem-
perament and a cultural background probably quite different
from yours, but God mediates truth through personality, so
I trust that some of the things he has taught me may be of
use to you.

Value of self-discipline

If you have planned your preaching you will, of course, be
relieved of that agonizing search for a text. What you will
preach on this week has already been decided. All you need
to do is to discipline yourself to work on the passage until
it yields its precious truths. Did I say 'all you need'? This
discipline is the hardest battle of sermon preparation. To
illustrate the value of such discipline let me give a word of
testimony.

As a young minister I was expected to preach one Sunday
at a youth service to which young people from seven years
and upwards would come. The reading given for that Sunday
in our denominational plan of readings was Luke 14:25–33.
How could I speak to such young children from such a
passage about hating father or mother? Yet I had no peace
to move from that text, either then at the beginning of the
week, or later when, conscious of the unsuitability, I des-
perately wanted to change. In the congregation on the
Sunday morning was a Christian nurse who had recently
led to Christ a woman from a very tough background.
Because of earlier drinking habits this woman still suffered

from depression. She had been depressed again on the day before the service, because her mother accused her of not showing love. 'You never take me for a drink now,' she said, 'you do not love me.' In fact the woman loved her mother now for the first time in her life. She could not stand the continual unjust accusation and had decided to abandon her Christian profession and to return to her old ways with her mother. 'Come to church just once more,' said the nurse. Reluctantly she came. When the Bible reading was announced she turned to the nurse and said, 'If he doesn't preach on that, I am through.' God's Spirit used a discipline to speak to a specific need and that person is now a Christian worker.

On another occasion in Australia I was asked to preach on Acts 19:1–22 and particular reference was made to Paul's handkerchiefs being used to cure sicknesses. I would not have chosen that particular passage, but as I prepared, I began to discover a wonderful pattern or strategy in church-planting was emerging. I did not recommend the use of handkerchiefs in healing and I doubt if Paul suggested the idea in the first place, but the need for confrontation with the powers of darkness is as relevant in church-planting today as it was then. What began as a tough assignment ended as a rich feast.

How to prepare an expository sermon

How then should you tackle the passage of Scripture before you?

1. Study the passage thoroughly and soak yourself in its contents
Commentaries at this stage stifle your thinking and cramp your mind to think just as the commentator does. This limits the Spirit of God. Once you have the passage in your mind you can meditate upon it on various occasions during the week, for instance, walking along the street or waiting at bus stops. I suggest not when crossing the road! Coming back for small periods again and again often produces more valuable thought than persevering through one long stretch.

This means, of course, starting early in the period available. One very fine expositor would roughly outline a message just as soon as he was invited to give it, even if the time of delivery was some way ahead. He could then spend any spare moments turning the passage over in his mind. By long exposure to thought and meditation the passage becomes part of you and speaks to your heart. Then the Spirit of God can put in your heart the particular application to the circumstances of your hearers. If you have studied a passage already in your morning devotions you will already have a series of notes available.

2. Write out an analysis of the passage

I mention this as something that I find very valuable. I am not suggesting that it is the only way to proceed, but I do find that it helps me to get right into the meaning of the passage and to appreciate its relevance to everyday life.

What I do is to write out the passage on the left-hand side of a piece of paper, leaving the right-hand side for later comments. In writing out the passage I think about the phrases and sentences and analyse their structure. I am alert to words and phrases that depend upon each other or that limit or enlarge upon the meaning. As I write I indent some of these words and phrases to show clearly this relationship. I am also aware of words or phrases on which I will later wish to comment on the right-hand side of the page.

Let me illustrate from a very familiar passage in John 3. The first verse reads, 'Now there was a man of the Pharisees named Nicodemus, a member of the ruling council.' I would write that verse in this way:

Now there was a man
       of the Pharisees
       named Nicodemus
       a member of the ruling council

'Now there was a man' is the basic statement. All the other phrases add to the picture presented of that man. Each one tells us more about him. So I indent each phrase to the same extent and place them one under the other.

The second verse reads, 'He came to Jesus at night and

said, "Rabbi, we know you are a teacher who has come
from God. For no one could perform the miraculous signs
you are doing if God were not with him." '
I would write that down as follows:

He came to Jesus
                at night
and said,
                'Rabbi,
                we know you are a teacher
                who has come from God
                for no one could perform the miraculous
                signs you are doing if God were not with
                him.'

I place his 'coming' and 'speaking' on the extreme left-hand
side as these are main verbs telling me not only who
Nicodemus is (which verse 1 has already told me) but the
things he did. 'At night' fills in more about when he came
and thereby tells me something of his feelings and motives.

What Nicodemus said I indent slightly. Basically he acknowledged Jesus politely by calling him 'Rabbi', he declared
his conviction about him and he gave a reason for that conviction. 'Who has come from God' adds something to the
thought of Jesus being a teacher. The rest of the sentence
is all of one piece explaining why Nicodemus had arrived
at his conclusion. Space, however, prevents it all being
placed on one line.

When I have written out the passage on the left-hand side
of the page I proceed to the right-hand side. Here, through
thought and prayer, meditation and study, I record those
things which arise from each sentence or phrase and which
I feel to be significant. They may add to my knowledge,
apply the wording to modern circumstances, draw a spiritual
conclusion, or in any other way be relevant.

For example, against 'of the Pharisees' in verse 1 I might
write, 'a religious leader, law-keeper, zealous person'. Against
'a member of the ruling council' I would write, 'a significant
person of some standing'.

In the second verse, against 'He came to Jesus' I might
write, 'earnest enough to go looking for Jesus'. Against 'by
night' I would write, 'Was he afraid, or cautious? Even so, he
still came.'

So verse 1 would look something like Table II.

Table II. Analysis of John 3:1

Now there was a man	
of the Pharisees	a religious leader, law-keeper, zealous person
named Nicodemus	appears later John 7:50; 19:39
a member of the ruling council	a significant person of some standing

---

What I am doing through this process is building up a picture of the passage and its happenings. By this means I do not miss out on significant details and I am challenged to think through difficult points of exegesis. For instance, in studying John 3 I will have to decide what I believe Jesus meant when he spoke of being 'born of water and the Spirit' — no easy task. This is the point at which commentaries are invaluable.

I mentioned meditation as a part of this whole process. Meditation is, I believe, a lost art among evangelical Christians. By meditation I do not mean mystical contemplation that empties the mind of thought or concentrates on something like God's being or God's love. I mean that form of meditation that feeds upon the words of Scripture, allowing the mind to turn them over and over and the heart to absorb their teaching. Prayerful meditation concentrates the mind upon the message of the Word. It also talks to the passage and asks questions. Why does this passage put things this way and not that way? Would I have expressed myself in that way in those circumstances? How was he feeling when he said or heard those words? Just as a cow chews and chews and chews the cud and in the process transforms plain green grass into rich white milk, so meditation deepens and enriches our understanding of God's Word. The fruits of such meditation can be preserved by recording them on the right-hand side of the page.

3. Examine the passage for relevance to modern life
This may be second nature to you. On the other hand, as
I listen to sermons, generally the weakest point is the application to daily life. By going through the analysis looking
for points of contemporary relevance, you will be
consciously concentrating on them. You will also be pro-
viding yourself with material to use in the process of applying
the message later.

For example, in John 3:1 I note that a good religious
leader of some standing in society may still be a person who
is looking for spiritual reality. None of us has gone so far
that we do not need help. In fact Nicodemus had missed
out on some very basic truths. That is still relevant and
may be one of those things you will want to point out in
applying the message.

4. Examine the structure of the passage
The analysis outlined above takes you right into the heart
of the passage and surrounds you with its truth. You have
been walking in the forest, admiring the trees and soaking
up the atmosphere. Now it is time to look at the forest as a
whole, how it stands together, where you can go in and
come out and what are the main paths.

Some people may prefer to tackle this at the beginning
but, whichever order you follow, you do need to know the
structure of the passage at some point. That will tell you
how the argument moves from point to point and what is
major and what is minor. You will also avoid the danger
of majoring on the minor, or drawing wrong conclusions
from an unbalanced understanding of the whole.

John 3:1–15 structurally appears to me to be constructed
as follows:

a. The need of the new birth (vv. 1–3)
    Without it a person cannot *see* the kingdom of God.

b. The nature of the new birth (vv. 4–8)
    Not a physical repeat of birth (v. 4).
    Involves cleansing and new life (v. 5).
    Not surprising because like produces like (v. 6).
    Unseen yet real (v. 8).
    Intangible but powerful working of the Spirit (v. 8).

c. The means of the new birth
> Through the person of Christ, who alone can reveal it
> (vv. 10—13).
> Through the death of Christ, the crucified yet exalted
> Substitute and Saviour (v. 14).
> Through the response of trust and committal (v. 15).

This structure will not necessarily govern the shape or points of your message. On many occasions it will, but not necessarily so. It will certainly assist in understanding the passage.

5. Find the main message of the passage
Ask yourself, 'What is the main thrust of this word to today's people and what points must be emphasized to bring home that main thrust to men's hearts?'

These points *must arise* from the text or passage, otherwise you are imposing your view, not expounding God's. If that is the case, then, however sound your teaching may be, it will not and cannot carry the authority of the Word of God with it.

No doubt you will have heard some wonderful exhortations to evangelism based on 2 Corinthians 4:3: 'If our gospel is veiled, it is veiled to those who are perishing.' Usually we are told that, unless we evangelize, we are veiling the gospel from the lost and if they never believe then it will be our fault and responsibility. In actual fact, Paul is telling us here that the veil actually lies in the minds of the unbelievers and the enemy has put it there. The veil is not under our control at all. Only God can remove it by his creative word that brings light in darkness even as he did in creation. Therefore the verse is not a challenge to evangelism, but the statement of a problem followed by an encouragement to persevere.

The main thrust of 2 Corinthians 4:1—6 is summed up in verse 1: 'We do not lose heart.' The other verses give the reasons for encouragement to persevere.

How to organize your material

1. Make your points clear and relevant
'The ontological argument for creation' may arise from a

text, but it will turn off the keenest congregation as quickly as a power failure turns out a light. You must not just ask, 'What does this say?' but 'What does this say to these people?' Your points must be *clear*. The congregation should be able to tell you the substance of those points at the end of the message. The test of teaching is whether the pupil learned, not whether the teacher covered his material. Clarity communicates.

2. Present your main points in a logical manner
They should be related. This relation may not be the relation of points in a straight line. They may be the relation of parts of a picture. But they should be related. Here there are basic differences in various cultures and languages. Western thought usually moves in a straight line, building up to a climax. Eastern thought and certainly Chinese language builds blocks into a total picture. Each part of a Chinese character adds something to the total meaning of a word. One character therefore may convey a total picture made up of different parts that in English would require a sentence to describe. 安 means peace. What is peace? English language would require even a paragraph to elaborate. By portraying one woman under one roof, Chinese has conveyed at least one meaning of peace by using two idea blocks that flash a pictorial message immediately. Similarly, Western preaching builds in a straight line to a climax, but Chinese preaching often uses several pictures or idea-blocks that communicate a message. The point I would stress here, however, is that the main points of the message, whether presented in Eastern or Western style, should be *clearly related both to the text and to each other*.

3. Stress your main points
Furthermore, if the main points are memorable they are more likely to be remembered! Some preachers have used alliteration so much that people are tired of it. Others have forced on main points headings that do not really fit. On the other hand, some can use clear headings naturally without making them sound forced and people find them easy to remember. Psalm 19, for example, divides very easily into three clear parts and these could well be headed: 1. God

speaks through the universe (vv. 1—6); 2. God speaks through his Word (vv. 7—10); 3. God speaks to the heart (vv. 12—13). Verse 14 then provides a closing prayer in the light of God's speaking.

How to develop the main points of your message

You know the broad outline, but much remains to be filled in. God speaks through the universe, but what do you need to say about that? Verses 1—4 of Psalm 19 speak of God revealing his glory and his work through the universe. This revelation is poured forth and is continuous, twenty-four hours a day (v. 2). It is a silent witness and yet a spoken one and it is a universal witness (vv. 3, 4). Take the following steps to develop your main points:

1. Ask yourself whether you need to emphasize all these truths to achieve your aim
Television adverts manage to convey a message in thirty seconds by ruthlessly cutting out all material not absolutely necessary. You could make a whole message from the first four verses of Psalm 19 by themselves, so if you are covering the whole psalm you will have to limit your material on the first section. Otherwise you will lose both your sense of direction and your congregation. Most of us try to say too much. Our hearers' ability to receive is usually far less than our desire to give.

2. Write down your thoughts in line with your aim
When you are developing your points and fitting the flesh to the skeleton outline you will probably find, as I do, that to write down your thoughts is necessary. For many people, writing stimulates thinking.

3. Build up to a climax that emphasizes your aim and then be prepared for a quick end
Too often a good message is ruined by a wandering finish. We shall consider the conclusion in a separate chapter, but for the moment note the need to work steadily up to a climax, reach it and stop. The course of your sermon, if plotted on a graph, should look roughly like the graph.

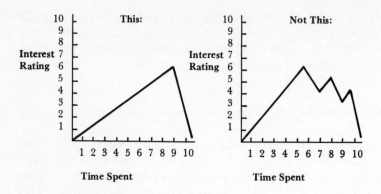

4. Decide how much or how little time you can give to each part and keep to that

Very often the second point of the sermon will bear more exposition than the first or last. If you spend too long on the first point the hearers may begin to wonder just when it will all end. In that case by the time the second section is finished the hearers may have had almost as much as they can take. But the middle section can stand longer time. In Psalm 19 this fits very well, for you would want to spend more time on revelation through God's Word than on the more general revelation conveyed by creation.

Verses 7–10 of Psalm 19 contain many explanations of what exactly the revealed Word of God does for the responsive person. The contrast between the clarity of this revelation and the indirectness portrayed in verses 1–4 tells us we need to spend more time expounding verses 7–10.[1]

5. Rely upon the Holy Spirit during delivery

There will be times when the Holy Spirit will take charge and you will abandon everything that you have prepared. You must not be so bound to your outline that you cannot respond to such prompting. On the other hand, of course, the Spirit's overruling must not be made an excuse for no or poor preparation.

6. Arrange the order of presentation of your points for maximum impact

I find that some people think that expository preaching is simply going through a passage verse by verse and commenting on each one. That can be both mechanical and boring. Psalm 19 lends itself to moving through the psalm in the order in which it is written, climaxing in the application of the revelation to the heart. Another passage may lend itself to reaching the climax in the central section of the passage, in which case you may abandon the order 1, 2, 3 and change it to 1, 3, 2. This is perfectly legitimate provided that you are not changing the thrust of the passage as it stands in the Bible.

7. Use parallel scriptures carefully

We live in a day when few Western Christians know their way around the Bible. Therefore if you are constantly referring them to other scriptures many will get lost or embarrassed. I therefore tend to use parallel scriptures very sparingly, unless the reference is going to be fairly extensive and I can guide my hearers carefully. I find that many preachers fly from one part of the Bible to another while missing out vital sections and truths in the passage in front of them. This indicates a fear of running out of material and that in turn shows a lack of deep preparation. So I suggest a sparing use of cross-references.

Study questions

1. Listen to someone preach. Try to decide what is his main aim and what are the main points of his message. How do they link together? If you can do this with a friend, check afterwards what in fact the main points and aim were.
2. Write out the main aim and main points for a sermon on the prodigal son (Luke 15:11–32).
3. What was the main aim of Jesus' message to the disciples in John 14:12–31? Trace his thought as it moves from point to point. How did he fulfil his aim?
4. You are preparing a message on Psalm 19. Your second point is 'God speaks through his Word.' Write out notes for what you would say under this heading, based on verses 7–10.

1. See Appendix A for analysis of Psalm 19.

6.
The exposition of narrative (or stories)

A personal communication

The Bible is full of stories, true accounts of happenings in time, space and history. They are some of the most wonderful stories in the world and all the more so because they are truth and not fiction.

God's revelation of himself to man has not been clothed in a series of philosophical or theological propositions, but in personal terms. He revealed himself through the lives of people and their experiences of him. He did not, for instance, leave us a lecture on the life of faith, but he did deal with Abraham in such a way that we have a living example of the life of faith before us. Bible stories, therefore, are not simply stories, but accounts of God's dealings with men and women.

God's revelation, especially in the early stages, is as much by act as word. Yet the word is needed to interpret the acts. At this point, God does present us with propositional truth. Some modern theologians will accept God's acts, but cannot accept the Word that explains them.

Yet very often we cannot understand what an act is all about unless it is accompanied by the word of explanation. So act and word go along together in the Bible. Sacrifices, for instance, would be senseless slaughter if God had not told us that 'Without the shedding of blood there is no forgiveness' of sins (Heb. 9:22).

Psalm 103:7 records, 'He made known his ways to Moses, his deeds to the people of Israel.' Moses had close access to God and, whereas all the people could see what God did, Moses was privileged to learn why he did it and what he meant. God's works illustrate God's ways and his ways interpret his works.

This is one reason why Scripture is so fascinating. The works of Scripture are displayed on the stage of human life and the words of Scripture are a God-given commentary on human life in relation to God. Revelation is not divorced from life and expressed in academic terms. Some of the words of Scripture arise from the deepest experiences of the human heart.

More than good stories

Because God has revealed himself in acts and words, the narratives of the Bible are very important. They are much more than good stories of historical accounts. They contain within themselves a revelation by God himself of his own character and of his will for men.

'Everything that was written in the past was written to teach us, so that through endurance and the encouragement of the Scriptures we might have hope' (Rom. 15:4). God guided the preparation of the Scriptures towards a particular end. He made sure by his Holy Spirit that what was recorded is effective and profitable for both endurance and encouragement, to enable Christians to remain firm under all circumstances and to strengthen their hope. The word for 'encouragement' comes from the same root as that used by Jesus to describe the Holy Spirit as the 'Counsellor' in John 15:26; 16:7. God himself is called 'the God who gives endurance and encouragement' in the very next verse (Rom. 15:5), thereby underlining that the words of Scripture are not simply words of good advice, but words which carry the power and authority of the living God and of his Holy Spirit.

Purpose of biblical narrative

Scripture, then, is a kind of divine casebook, in which human circumstances, fears, hopes, failings and anxieties are expressed in living examples and God's answers to human problems live before our eyes. Paul in writing to the Corinthians outlines the story of the exodus from Egypt and then

declares that 'These things occurred as examples, to keep
us from setting our hearts on evil things as they did,' and
that 'These things happened to them as examples and were
written down as warnings for us, on whom the fulfilment
of the ages has come' (1 Cor. 10:6, 11). Scripture narrative
is not meant to be just a good story, but an educational
guide in the school of life. The stories of Scripture are
therefore as vital to our instruction as the passages of doctrine. They clothe the truth in flesh and blood and make
it easier for us to understand.

In accordance with this way of presenting truth, John
describes Jesus' miracles not simply as wonders, but as
'signs', carrying a much deeper meaning than an isolated
set of marvellous actions could possibly do. Modern television has learned from the biblical method. Some of the
most popular programmes are series on the lives and actions
of one family or set of characters. By embodying certain
ideas in these characters, the broadcaster communicates
to the receiver the emotions and reactions he wants that
receiver to experience. The aim may be to alert the viewer
to the danger of drugs or the effects of pollution. Indeed,
the object may be openly political, but the end is not
achieved by a direct approach. Instead, a story lived out on
the screen shows the positive and negative results of these
things in human lives. The audience then becomes
emotionally involved.

Nathan succeeded in using this method with David (2 Sam.
12:1—10). Instead of preaching to David on the evil of
adultery, Nathan told him the story of the rich man who
robbed a poor man of his pet lamb in order to provide a
feast for the rich man's guests. David became so emotionally
involved that he wanted to kill the rich man. Nathan had
made his point and all he needed to do was to say, 'You
are the man,' for David to be convicted to his heart.

In East Asia, the wayang play or Chinese opera have been
used like this for centuries and they still draw the crowds.
How sad then that we use Bible stories so little in both east
and west, especially those stories of the Old Testament!
Indeed, to many the Old Testament is a closed book. Yet
a church that is not taught in the Old Testament usually
has a weak idea of the greatness, majesty and holiness of

God and is liable to be shallow in its approach to evangelism. We neglect Bible stories at our peril.

Using biblical narratives for expository preaching

How then do you deal with a story for preaching purposes? The first things you do are to
1. think yourself into the circumstances of the story;
2. use your imagination;
3. live out the drama in your own mind;
4. imagine how each of the characters must have been feeling at different times;
5. ask yourself why the characters acted or reacted as they did and what they felt like as they did it.

A story that has never lived for you will never live for your hearers. One of the most memorable sermons I have heard was on the healing of the paralysed man let down through the roof. The preacher saw the miracle of healing through the eyes of four different people, pictured in his imagination as the four men who carried the sick man. What they felt was derived from the truths of the passage, but the result of using this method was that all of us could identify in our thoughts and emotions with these different men. Remember that although our outward living conditions may be different from those of biblical days, men still have the same desires, fears, hopes, ambitions and sorrows. The human condition never changes, nor does God.

Test your story-telling talent

A good exercise in testing yourself on your ability to make stories live is to tell them or read them to children. Children love stories and react spontaneously with interest or boredom, so they give a more honest response. Training yourself to be responsive and sensitive to children's reactions is a wonderful preparation and discipline for a preacher.

Probing questions

Having soaked yourself in the atmosphere of a story until
you can see the glint of the sun on Goliath's spear, or touch
the hem of Jesus' robe in the crowd, begin to ask yourself
these questions:
1. Who are the main people involved?
2. What can I discover about the attitudes, motives,
   thoughts and reactions of each person?
3. What is the main aim of the story in this context?
4. What is the context in which this story appears in the
   Scripture?

An example of the importance of the context comes in
Matthew 22:41—46. Jesus asked a question of the Pharisees
about the Christ being the son of David. This story cannot
be rightly understood except in the light of the searching
questions the lawyers and Sadducees had been asking Christ.
Seen in that context, Jesus' question brilliantly stopped all
argument, silenced the opposition and boldly claimed his
own divinity. His enemies had no answer and their enforced
silence said more than hours of teaching could possibly have
done.

How to prepare a biblical narrative for exposition

Let me now illustrate the method of preparing a biblical
narrative for exposition using Mark 12:41—44.

An analysis of the passage as suggested in the previous
chapter helps to discover what you are looking for. An
analysis of the passage would look something like Table III.

You now have plenty of material to use, and the story of
the poor widow and her two coins can be looked at like this:

1. The context
Jesus disputed with the Pharisees and condemned them for
making too much of religious actions and too little of heart
motives.

2. The main people involved
Jesus, the rich people, the poor widow.

Table III. Analysis of Mark 12:41—44

v. 41 Jesus sat down	A deliberate act.
opposite the place where the offerings were put	A special place.
and watched the crowd putting their money into the temple treasury	He noticed and cared.
Many rich people	The majority is not always right.
threw in	Ostentation.
large amounts.	Big money.
v. 42 But a poor widow	The poorest class.
came and	She came too.
put in two	Small amount
very small copper coins,	of small change,
worth only a fraction of a penny.	of little worth.
v. 43 Calling his disciples to him,	A lesson to teach.
Jesus said, 'I tell you the truth	Strong emphasis.
this poor widow	The least noticed.
has put more into the treasury than all the others.	Value in giving.
v. 44 They all gave out of their wealth;	Still plenty left.
but she, out of her poverty,	Nothing left.
put in everything —	Gave her all,
all she had to live on.'	even her necessity.

3. What can be learnt from each person?

From Jesus we can learn that God looks upon things differently from the way men do. He deliberately placed himself where he could see what was happening and he noticed what no one else seems to have seen. His assessment of human actions goes right to the heart of the matter. He also wanted his disciples to learn from the incident, so called them across to watch and to hear his comments. He underlined the importance of the lesson by the words with which he introduced it.

From the rich people we can see how easy it is to look for approval from others and to assess our standing from it. The opening of the chest in the treasury made it possible to make a great noise in throwing money against the metal, so that a rich man could create quite an impression by using the right coins.

From the widow we can learn that the Lord notices things that other people ignore. Giving is not assessed in terms of what we give, but in terms of what we have left afterwards. She, no doubt, felt that she had nothing to give, but in the end she outgave them all. Motive in this connection is more important than money.

Now you are in the position to answer the question: 'What is the main aim of the story?' You have to think this through carefully. I discovered two possible main aims for this story. They should be thought of as alternatives rather than trying to use both of them at the same time. One of the aims could be to illustrate how God looks on the heart and not on the appearance. The other could be to show that when we give to God it is not what we have given, but what we have left that counts. You would decide which aim to pursue and use your material accordingly.

Sermon outline on Mark 12:41–44

The following is a possible outline for a sermon with the first of these aims in mind. It is not developed but set out in a bare outline that would obviously need much work done on it, and it would also need introducing and finishing off.

1. The care and concern of the Lord
Jesus noticed the poor widow.
No one is too poor, too weak or too old to matter.
Those whom men ignore, the Lord is aware of.
The Lord was there deliberately watching not just how much
    people gave, but the motive with which they gave.
Few people would have noticed Jesus' presence.
The Lord is still present and concerned today.

2. The judgement men made

Everyone noticed the rich people and their giving.

By throwing coins against the brass opening of the chest they could create quite an impression.

There were many rich people doing this.

No doubt they did actually put in large sums of money.

Hardly anyone would have noticed the insignificant widow.

Men judge on outward appearances.

3. The judgement God made

The Lord noticed the individual person.

He assessed her gift as the most valuable because
  — they gave out of their riches,
  — she gave out of her poverty,
  — she gave until she had nothing left.

God measures according to motive as much as or more than by the amount.

God looks on the heart, but man on the outward appearance.

Conclusion to be drawn

Every person and every act is significant in God's sight.

God looks on the heart and the motive and that is what should govern our giving, responding in love to him.

We must be careful lest we judge according to man's judgement and miss out on that which is really significant.

When giving to God we should measure what is left, not what is given.

The parts of this message can be expanded but, of course, you must be careful about how much time you give to each. Do not spend so much time on the first parts that you do not have enough time left to reach the main point that you intend to pass on.

Almost any narrative can be dealt with using this approach, whether from the Old or New Testament. By writing down your thoughts and meditations, you make them clear and firm. Writing them down also often leads to new thoughts coming to mind. Narratives are the easiest passages to bring alive to a congregation. People are interested in people and can identify with them, so we should make maximum use of the stories of people that God has provided for us in the Scriptures.

Study questions

1. Write out Mark 10:46–52 as suggested in this chapter. Then fill in the right-hand column and from this pick out what would be your main headings for a message.
2. Read a passage from a classical or modern story book to a friend or into a tape recorder. Ask your friend to comment on, or ask yourself the following:
   Does this story live, the way I read it?
   Does the tone of my voice vary or is it monotonous?
   How could I make this sound more interesting?
3. Tell the story of Zacchaeus (Luke 19:1–10) as though it happened last week in your town, using modern equivalents.
4. Describe exactly how Peter and John individually felt when they went into the tomb and discovered that Jesus' body was not there.

7.
Exposition of the psalms

One of the saddest lacks in the church today is our failure to make adequate use of the psalms. When did you last hear an exposition of the psalms and when did you last speak from a psalm? I think you will find that it is quite hard to remember when. Yet the psalms are a treasury of devotion and worship, and of human experience without parallel anywhere in the world.

The psalms have been described as the hymn book of Israel, for they were written to be sung. Like all good hymns they express particular experiences in general terms, so that, although we may not be facing the particular experience, we can share in the feelings of the psalmist and identify with him. Perhaps I can illustrate what I mean from the hymn which begins, 'O love that will not let me go.' This hymn arose out of the particular experience of George Matheson. He was engaged to be married, but then began to go blind. His fiancée decided that she could not go through with the marriage, and he was left terribly disappointed. He found consolation in the love of the Lord, who would not let him go, and in renewed dedication of himself to that Lord. Many people who sing that hymn today know nothing of George Matheson's own experience. However, they have been able to identify with him because they have been facing other disappointments, such as failure to get a certain job, the failure of a close friend they are relying on for help, and so on. A good hymn will always have the power to speak from a particular problem to many other problems.

In the psalms, there is scarcely any human emotion or experience that is not expressed. Our systems of theological education tend to concentrate on the academic training of the mind. Most ordinary people, however, tend to operate

more on the level of their feelings. There should be good
reason, therefore, for them to be able to respond to the
expressions of feeling found in the psalms. Although they
may act as much from feelings as from anything that does
not mean, however, that they find it easy either to understand their feelings or to express them. When therefore they
find someone expressing how they are feeling, then they
can identify with that person. In the psalms, sorrow, bitter-
ness, fear, depression, hope, frustration, vindication and joy
are all found movingly expressed. The deep penitence of
Psalm 51 is balanced by the joyous praise of Psalm 150.
The depression of Psalm 42 is balanced by the confidence
of Psalm 107. The book therefore offers a rich mine from
which to quarry sermons, enabling people to understand and
express their emotions and enabling the preacher to identify
with them in those emotions, as he, too, is human.

A poetic form

In tackling the psalms we must recognize that they are
hymns and they are poetry. Hence, we must understand
something about Hebrew poetry. Every country has its own
poetic forms, not readily understood by people from a
different culture. Hebrew poetry is no exception. Western
poetry until quite recently was based on rhyme and rhythm.
Hebrew poetry never was. Parallelism is the basis of Hebrew
poetry. The way it works is that an idea is expressed in a
certain way in one line. Then the idea may be repeated in
the next line in different words, or contrasted with another
opposite idea, or developed further in another direction, or
followed through to completion. The second line again may
be related to the first as effect is related to cause. Let me
illustrate. 'Increase the days of the king's life,' is the first
line of Psalm 61:6 and the second line repeats the thought
by adding, 'His years for many generations'. The basic
thought is the same, but it is expressed in different words.
Psalm 110:5 develops the thought of the first line in the
second one:
>   'The Lord is at your right hand;
>   he will crush kings on the day of his wrath. '

In the same psalm the second line of verse 7 is the effect that flows from the first line:
'He will drink from a brook beside the way;
    therefore he will lift up his head.'

Understanding how Hebrew poetry works provides help in understanding the message of a psalm.

Guidelines in expounding psalms

1. Find out as much as possible about the experience that lies behind the psalm
If you know what the psalmist was facing, then you have a much clearer idea of the full meaning of his words.

Psalm 51 becomes much more meaningful when you realize that this is David's confession of sin after his adultery with Bathsheba and his murder of Uriah the Hittite. This psalm is without parallel in showing what true repentance and confession really mean. You do not have to limit its application to sexual sins, because repentance is basically the same for any sin and everyone needs true repentance if he is ever to prosper in the Christian life.

Psalm 3 is clearly the expression of a man surrounded by enemies and tempted to despair and fear. The heading of the psalm suggests that at this particular time David was fleeing the kingdom after the rebellion of his son Absalom. Knowing that makes the feelings he expressed even more moving, but you can apply the message of the psalm to any modern situation where troubles abound and seem insurmountable and where it is hard to sleep at night for worrying about them.

Not all of the psalms can be traced to particular incidents. Many of them are the experiences of Israel as a nation and can be applied to groups rather than individuals, but where a historical background is brought to our attention or is pretty clear from the wording of the psalm, we have the possibility of deep enrichment.

2. Discover where possible the separate stanzas that go to make up the psalm.
Again, this is not always possible because some of the psalms

do not appear to have been written in this way, but where the stanzas can be identified you have a great help to clearer exegesis. Some Bibles are printed with the psalms so divided up. Of course, the Hebrew stanzas do not in any way coincide with the division into verses in our Bibles, but are rather several verses put together.

Psalm 1 clearly divides into two stanzas, the one drawing a picture of the godly righteous man and the other a picture of the ungodly. The two stanzas stand in direct contrast to each other and in this case give a very clear distinction to be used in constructing the points of your sermon.

3. Study the problem that faced the psalmist and find out all you can about how he tackled the problem

How, for example, did he find help in God? What did he ask for? What truths about God himself did he find helpful to him? What was the end result of the action he took?

In Psalm 3 the problem faced by David was that of a great many enemies, who were rising up against him and most of whom had written him off as being beyond the help even of God. He tackled the problem in his own heart by thinking upon God as his shield, his glory and his vindicator. He turned all this into prayer, in confidence that God would answer, and the practical results were a good night of sleep (which, no doubt, he needed) and an ability to face an overwhelming enemy without the paralysing effect of fear. In fact, we know that eventually he was restored to his kingdom. The important point for a message, however, is the practical effect of meditating on the power of God to keep us and the power of prayer to settle our minds, however great our problems in life. Prayer in this context is the secret to a good night's sleep in the midst of worry, to a heart at peace in the midst of violent opposition.

4. Relate the particular problem of the psalmist to the present problems of your own congregation

None of them are kings who have been put off their thrones by a *coup d'état*, but quite a number of them are surrounded by so many difficulties that they probably feel that even God cannot help them out of them. Some of the people may not be sleeping too well, and a message on this psalm could make all the difference to them as the Holy Spirit applies the Word to their hearts.

At times you will realize that the psalmist himself has not found his way through to the answer. The psalm may leave many questions unanswered, but this in itself is so true to life. The Lord never promised that we would always have quick, easy answers to our problems or that we would never have outstanding questions to which we do not have an answer. To be honest and share with your congregation that this is not only true, but is the universal experience of the people of God down the ages, can encourage them to know that their experience is not unique.

Practical application

Once again, I have often found it helpful to write out an analysis of the psalm (Table IV), keeping the right-hand column free for noting what I have learnt from the text and only using that column after completing the left-hand one. As an exercise you might like to cover the right-hand column with a piece of blank paper and write down what you learn alongside the writing in the left-hand column, before comparing your thinking with mine. I have taken Psalm 95 because this is a psalm about worship that is very relevant to our subject.

An interpretation

As I looked again over what I had written down, I realized that the psalm falls naturally into three stanzas, one of which begins in the middle of one of our verse divisions. The *first section*, from verses 1–5, is an invitation to worship God in praise, joy, even a joyful noise, singing and thanksgiving, simply because he is God who made the world and keeps it going. This is a general invitation to all to worship their Creator and such worship is meant to be a joyful occasion. The *second section* is in a quieter key, calling for humble adoration and bent knees. The invitation here is more personal and limited to those who can say that the

Table IV. Analysis of Psalm 95

v. 1 Come, let us sing for joy to the Lord; let us shout aloud to the Rock of our salvation.	Joyous singing, directed to the Lord. Loud noise of praise, directed to the solid hope.
v. 2 Let us come before him with thanksgiving and extol him with music and song.	Worship is before God Thanksgiving for his gifts.
v. 3 *For* the Lord is the great God the great King above all gods.	*Reason* for praise is the greatness and rule of God.
v. 4 In his hand are the depths of the earth, and the mountain peaks belong to him.	He is the Creator. Heights and depths
v. 5 The sea is his, for he made it, and his hands formed the dry land.	mighty seas, dry land — all made by him.
v. 6 Come, let us bow down in worship, let us kneel before the Lord our Maker;	Humble attitude to give worth to God Reverence before the Eternal, before the Creator.
v. 7 *For* he is our God and we are the people of his pasture, the flock under his care Today, if you hear his voice,	Personal relationship. *Reason* for adoration. Personal shepherding. The most important day. We worship, God speaks.
v. 8 do not harden your hearts as you did at Meribah, as you did that day at Massah in the desert,	Warning to listeners. Lesson from Exodus 17:1—7. Learn from the past.
v. 9 where your fathers tested and tried me, though they had seen what I did.	Refusal to listen and obey. Despite all evidence.

Table IV (cont'd).

v.10	For forty years I was angry with that generation;	God's response.
	I said, 'They are people whose hearts go astray, and they have not known my ways.'	To refuse to listen is to go wrong.
v.11 So	I declared on oath in my anger, 'They shall never enter my rest.'	God's wrath. Man's punishment.

Lord is their God, they are his people and he is their Shepherd. Only the true believer who knows the great Shepherd of the sheep can possibly join in this kind of worship. Verses 6—7b cover this section. *The rest of the psalm* is very solemn indeed and has reference to hearing God speak to the congregation, warning them that they should listen carefully and not in any way harden their hearts. The stern lesson of Israel in the wilderness is put before them. Their obedience and response to the Word of God now determines their future enjoyment of God's blessings.

I found in this psalm a pattern for worship, including singing, thanksgiving and praise, prayer, adoration and quiet worship and then, finally, the ministry of the Word of God. It is interesting to note here, too, that listening to the Word of God is not an added extra to the rest of the service, nor does it take up nearly all the time, but it is an important part in a balanced diet of worship, whereby God may speak to us as well as our speaking to him. Maintaining this balance is never easy. Some churches confine the preacher to ten minutes, as though the sermon were a tolerated nuisance, while others expect the preacher to begin after a hymn and prayer hastily disposed of, as though God were not worthy of our best offering of praise and adoration.

The important point, however, is that the setting out of a psalm like this can help you to see what the structure of it is and what lessons you can gain from it. You will notice the way I have deliberately listed the 'let us' phrases one under the other. This helps towards clear comparison. You will notice too that I have put the words 'for' and 'so' in italics. That is because these are important link words in Scripture giving us reasons why certain things follow each other. The reference to Exodus 17, of course, opens another whole sphere for illustrating the dangers of disobeying the Word of God. You have to decide how much or how little of the detail of that illustration you want to, or have time to use. Again, you will almost certainly have far too much material for one sermon in the psalm and you have the difficult task of deciding what to leave out in order to express the main theme of the psalm or the part of it on which you will preach.

The psalms touch the devotional heart of the Word of God. If you can introduce your people to these songs and give them a taste of what it means to identify with the joys and sufferings, hopes and fears of the people who wrote them, you will have done a deep service to the people of God in our day.

Study questions

1. Analyse Psalm 67 according to the suggested pattern and outline a message on the psalm.
2. What kind of circumstances do you think caused Psalms 53, 73 and 115 to be written?
3. In Psalm 121 what are modern equivalents in our experience of 'the hills' of verse 1, the 'shade' of verse 5, the thoughts expressed in verse 6 and the 'coming and going' of verse 8?

8.
Expounding the epistles

A challenging expository subject

The letters of the New Testament present the most rewarding
and yet challenging parts of the Scriptures for the expositor.
The problem is not so much what to say as what to leave out,
and how to do justice to a passage packed with rich material.
The mind of a man like Paul was so filled with ideas, and the
object of his thinking was so glorious and abounding that,
as Peter himself confessed in a major understatement, 'His
letters contain some things that are hard to understand.' Our
job is not only to understand as much as we can, but also to
communicate to our people in terms that they can understand and that are relevant to their daily lives. These letters
are often closely argued documents. They are full of detailed
truth and careful shades of meaning. In them every single
word is full of significance. Expounding them therefore
calls for hard work by the preacher before he can ever begin
to put a message together.

I have found the following principles very helpful in using
the epistles.

Guidelines in expounding the epistles

*1. Take note of the main verbs and the tenses used in these
verbs*
They are the action words and they govern the whole of the
rest of the sentence. In this connection a knowledge of the
original Greek is tremendously helpful. Greek was a much
more accurate language than English and capable of very
delicate shades of meaning. If you have not been able to

study Greek for yourself, check up, if you can, with the aid of suitable commentaries that will explain the important differences. Even if you cannot do that because you do not have commentaries available, do not give up on the epistles. There is still a wealth of spiritual truth available to you, but be sure to take notice of the verbs that are used. An example of the importance of verbal forms is in Ephesians 5:18: 'Be filled with the Spirit.' The command is not to have a once-for-all experience, but to be under the constant control of the Holy Spirit. As it is given as a command it is something for which we are responsible and not something that we have to wait for God to do for us.

2. Notice the positives and negatives that come in the passage
Scripture does not always define things positively. Sometimes we are told what is not right, or what something is not, rather than what it is, and this helps us in our understanding. Do not be afraid of the negatives. 1 Corinthians 13 is an example of this. Verses 4 to 6 read: 'Love is patient, love is kind' – a very positive statement, but then it goes on: 'It does not envy, it does not boast, it is not proud. It is not rude, it is not self-seeking, it is not easily angered, it keeps no record of wrongs. Love does not delight in evil, but rejoices with the truth.' An emphasis on the negative helps us to highlight the positive, just as a good negative in photography is necessary for a sharp final print. The epistles often place the negative and positive alongside each other, and we should take full account of this.

Another important feature of the epistles is the use of prepositions like 'in', 'by', 'with', 'to' and 'through'. Greek used many prepositions, in order to give fine shades of meaning. Some modern languages use many of them, but others use very few and if your own language is one of the latter, then you may need to give greater thought as to how to convey the meaning of the epistles to your hearers. You may also be tempted to overlook the importance of some of these words. Conjunctions are also very important, for they connect one line of argument with another. 'And', 'but', 'therefore', or 'because' can carry important meanings for the expositor.

3. Have the main theme of the passage clear in your mind before you begin to interpret the details

Otherwise you can misinterpret what the Scripture is really saying. This is particularly true when you are speaking on passages about which Christians are not completely agreed, such as those relating to disputable matters or to spiritual gifts (Rom. 14; 1 Cor. 12). A grasp of the main argument and an understanding of the problem with which the apostle was dealing will keep you from unbalanced presentations. Attention to the main verbs will help you again here, for they hold the whole passage together.

4. Know the circumstances of the people to whom the letter was written wherever that is possible

To know something of the Gnostic heresy that John was facing when he wrote his letters helps you to understand some of his wording. To know that Paul was tackling a situation where people were going back to salvation by works and law-keeping in Galatians helps you to understand why he wrote so strongly and why what he says may seem to contradict some of James' writing. In fact James was tackling the reverse situation, where people were relying on a head knowledge that produced no practical result in their lives.

5. Decide early on how you will approach the epistle

If you have unlimited time before you, you may want to preach through the epistle. But then this may take a matter of years, if you preach once a week and expound the details of the book. Most of us have neither the ability to sustain such a long series nor the congregation that will be content to listen, so you have to decide what main themes you will develop, or what parts you will leave out, or where you will stop and take some other subject. Consecutive preaching builds up the faith of the people, but there is no point in losing their interest by continuing with the same series too long. One of the hardest tasks of the preacher is choosing what treasures to leave out.

6. Keep a careful check on the subjects you choose, to ensure an adequate balance of teaching

One thing to beware of in taking an epistle is lest you always preach on the doctrinal part or always preach on the ethical part. Most of the epistles begin with doctrine and then lead on to the ethical results of such doctrines. To preach on the ethics without the doctrine is to leave ethics without any base, and to preach on doctrine without ethics is to leave doctrine in the air and unrelated to life on the shop-floor or in the market. All of us have our own pet themes and part of the value of exposition is to keep us from going back to them all the time.

7. *Follow the rules of biblical interpretation*

Such rules as not interpreting one passage of Scripture in a way that contradicts the plain teaching of another part are vital. A full list of such principles of interpretation is beyond the scope of this book. One thing, however, I would like to say. I find that many lay people come to the Bible with a conscious or unconscious feeling that because it is God's Word inspired by his Spirit, somehow the ordinary rules of language do not apply. If, therefore, I ask them what a particular verse says on some subject they will often ignore the plain meaning of the words and come out with some safe phrase that they remember about the gospel, such as, 'We must all believe in Jesus.' The verse may say nothing of the kind, but there seems to be an inbuilt feeling that the plain words cannot possibly mean what they actually say and there must be some deeper meaning known only to those who have studied for the ministry. Preachers have sometimes been responsible for this sad fact, because they have drawn somewhat fanciful pictures from passages that were never meant to say such things. Because the congregation cannot see the connection between the passage and the picture, they assume that there must be something wrong with the way they look at the Bible, instead of something being very wrong with the preacher. Our job, however, is not to make the plain meaning look difficult, but to make plainer that which is already plain and to send the congregation home feeling that they want to look at that passage again, because it has become so clear to them.

Practical application

Once again, in expounding the epistles, I have found it helpful to write out a passage with two columns (see Table V).
This time, because there is so much to be learnt from the
letters I have put fewer words on each line. You might like
to cover the right-hand column with a blank piece of paper
and see if you can receive help by jotting down your own
conclusions.

Because the epistles contain so much closely packed
material, you will find that you need more space in which
to write out your analysis. You will also do well to look
at the passage as a whole when you have written down the
left-hand side, before beginning to write anything on the
right. Some patterns may then emerge.

An interpretation

Let me now comment on this analysis. You will notice
first of all that by starting in from the margin it is com-
paratively easy to see the *main verbs*. You see here that
God has blessed us (v. 3), chosen us (v. 4), predestined us
(v. 5), freely given his glorious grace (v. 6) and made known
to us the mystery of his will (v. 9). As I discovered this,
on going down the right-hand column, I could see that an
outline for a sermon comes right away. The theme would
be 'The great things God has done for us.' The main sections
could be developed in terms of God's choice before the
foundation of the world, leading to our being holy and
blameless before him; God's predestining us, leading to our
being sons of God; God's making known to us, leading to
our sharing in what he is doing; and God's blessing us with
every spiritual blessing, leading us to have all that we need
to fulfil our destiny. Obviously there would be enough,
and more than enough, to keep us going for some time.

Then you will notice the *prepositions*. We are blessed
in Christ and *in* the heavenly realms. We are predestined
in love *through* Jesus Christ *in accordance with* his pleasure
and will. We have redemption *through* his blood, *in accordance with* the riches of his grace. All of these small words

Table V. Analysis of Ephesians 1:3—10

v. 3   Praise be to the God
                              and Father
                                          of our Lord
                                                      Jesus Christ,
                          who has blessed us
                              in the heavenly realms
                                          with every
                                                      spiritual blessing
                          in Christ.

v. 4   *For* he chose us
                              in him
                                          before the creation of the world.
                                          to be holy
                                              and blameless
                                                  in his sight.

   In love

v. 5   he predestined us
                                          to be adopted as his sons
                                  through Jesus Christ
                                          in accordance with his pleasure and will

v. 6   to the praise of his glorious grace,
                          which he has freely given us
                              in the One he loves.

v. 7   In him we have redemption
                                          through his blood,
                                          the forgiveness of sins,
                                          in accordance with the riches of God's
                                              grace

v. 8   that he lavished on us
                                          with all wisdom and understanding.

v. 9   And he made known to us
                                          the mystery of his will
                                          according to his good pleasure,
                                          which he purposed
                          in Christ

v.10   to be put into effect
                                          when the times will have reached
                                              their fulfilment —
                                          to bring all things
                                              in heaven and on earth together
                                              under one head,
                                  even Christ.

To Jesus as man, God is God. We are to praise him.
God is also Father of the Lord in every sense.
Jesus Christ is the supreme Lord.
He is also Saviour and Anointed One.
What God has done — blessed us
>   in the unseen yet real spiritual dimension;
>   in everything and with all we need.
>   These blessings are spiritual, related to our deepest need.
Everything is contained in Christ and our relationship to him.
What God has done in detail — chosen us.
Again this is done in Christ.
When he did it — before the world began.
Why he did it - for positive living, holy living, right living;
>   — for negative removal of blame for wrong living.
What happens in the sight of God is what is important.
The overwhelming motive of God is love.
What God has done in detail — destined us beforehand.
Why he did it — to adopt us into his family
Again, through Christ,
>   because God has chosen to do it that way.
This wonderful, undeserved love merits all our praise.
What God has done in detail — freely given his grace,
but again, only in Christ, the supreme object of his love.
Grace leads in Christ to redemption — purchase back.
>   Only available through the cross.
>   Involves and makes possible forgiveness of sins.
>   Proportionate to the richness of grace.

Grace is lavish
>   and manifests God's perfect wisdom and understanding.
What God has done in detail — revelation and manifestation.
A mystery is something previously hidden but now revealed.
Depends entirely upon his good pleasure
>   and deliberate purpose.
Again, all contained in Christ.
God's will must inevitably be accomplished,
>   but only at the absolutely right time.
>   This is ultimate fulfilment.
>   This aim is total integration of a disintegrated
>   universe, spiritual and earthly.
One central Head to this new fulfilment,
Jesus Christ himself.

add a new depth to our understanding of the love of God
towards us.

You may have noticed that time and time again God works
out all his purposes for us 'in Christ'. I had picked up that
recurring theme as I looked at the passage as a whole, and
therefore in my analysis I made sure that every time the
concept occurred I placed the words at the same point of
indentation from the margin. So I could readily pick out
from my analysis that we are blessed with every blessing
in Christ, chosen in Christ, predestined to be adopted
through Christ, receive God's glorious grace in him, find
redemption in him and see in him the fulfilment of all God's
plans and purposes for history. Here is the most wonderful
treasury of material for a message on our riches in Jesus
Christ.

I then noticed the reasons given for God pouring out his
grace upon us in Jesus Christ. Verse 4 tells us that his
intention in choosing us was to produce a people who would
live holy lives, lives in accordance with his will and purity.
Verse 5 tells us that he predestined us in order to adopt us
into his family, and verse 10 tells us that his final purpose
is to unite all of this disintegrating world under the headship
of Jesus Christ. In these three areas we find our significance,
we find our security, as he accomplishes his purposes and
none can stop him, and we find that we are the objects of
his never-failing love. If only men and women would see
just what God is like, they would soon abandon other ways
of satisfying basic God-implanted needs. These three
purposes of God therefore could form the basis of a message
that not only comes straight out of Ephesians, but applies
to the crying needs of modern men and women.

I also noticed in this passage that God chose us before
the creation of the world (v. 4). He was at work on our
behalf *before* history ever began. But verse 7 tells us that
through the cross we have redemption through the blood
of Christ, the forgiveness of our sins. He has been at work
during history. Verse 10 tells us that he intends to bring
all things together under the headship of Christ. He will
accomplish his purposes for us at the end of and *beyond*
history. What a wonderful picture this gives us of the love
and grace of our God! A message on this subject could be

of immense help to someone feeling as though life has
come to an end for him or her, or that there is no meaning
to it all.

By moving down the column again I discovered a contrast between the cost to man of this wonderful salvation
and the cost to Christ. For us there is the glorious grace
freely bestowed upon us in the Beloved. For him there
is the price of his blood so freely shed for us. This is not
a main theme of the passage and I would not take this
particular contrast as the basis for a sermon, but it might
be very helpful to draw attention to the contrast in the
process of developing one of the main themes of the
passage.

Sermon outline

The following might be the outline of a sermon based on
the main verbs of this passage:

1. God has chosen us
Verse 4 tells us how and when and why.
>   He chose us in Christ and we owe everything to him.
>   He chose us before the foundation of the world, when
>   we could have no part in it.
>   He chose us to be holy, whole, complete human beings
>   under his direction.
>   He chose us to be blameless, free from every accusation.

2. God has predestined us
Verse 5 tells us
>   that the context of this truth is in the love of God;
>   that it was with a view to adoption into his family;
>   that because the work is entirely God's and in accord-
>   ance with his good pleasure, we should worship and
>   adore and praise him.

3. God has freely given us his glorious grace
Verses 6, 7 tell us that that grace is completely free to us,
>   but that is because we have redemption through the
>   cost to his loved one of his shed blood.
>   This made possible the forgiveness of our sins.

4. God has made known to us the mystery of his will

Verses 9, 10 explain how what God has done and is doing
for us is all in the context of a world-wide, history-
long plan for the whole universe

and one day it will be all gathered together under the
headship of Jesus Christ.

No wonder, then, that Paul begins this passage by praising
God and saying that God has blessed us with every spiritual
blessing in Christ.

This is, of course, the barest of outlines and, as I wrote
it, I was conscious of the vast amount of material contained
in it. Very careful selection would need to be made of the
points to be expanded. You will notice also that no introduction is mentioned, because that is dealt with elsewhere.
The point I want to make, however, is that these great
truths are there in the Scriptures and they only need drawing
out and putting before us in order to come to life, and that
is our job as preachers of the Word.

Study questions

1. Prepare an outline of a message on justification by faith
   from Romans 5:1—11.
2. What were the circumstances behind John's Second and
   Third Epistles, as far as you can tell from the letters
   themselves, without the help of commentaries?
3. List the main verbs of 1 Timothy 4:6—16. What do you
   need to do in the light of these verbs to make yourself a
   more effective preacher? Express this in terms of
   practical decision to be acted upon.
4. How would you plan a series of messages on a long book
   like Romans?

9.
Expounding the prophets

A difficult but rewarding expository subject

If the epistles present the most rewarding and challenging section of the Scriptures for the expositor, the prophets represent the most difficult part. They spoke to a situation that was so different from ours, as far as outward circumstances are concerned, and used such different language forms from our everyday speech that we find them very hard to follow. But we are told that all Scripture is inspired by God and is profitable, and when we get behind the prophets and into them we find some of the most up-to-date messages from God to us.

We must remember that a prophet was not primarily someone who foretold what was going to happen, but someone who told forth what God thought about what was actually happening when he spoke. The prophets are God's commentary on the religious, social, moral and political life of the time. Inasmuch as man is still the same in himself and still faces problems in ordering his society, the prophets still provide a commentary that is relevant today. Sometimes people complain that Christians have nothing to say about the problems of society. That was never true with the prophets and if we faithfully expound them we shall have something to say, too.

In Amos 8:5 the prophet complains against the materialistic businessman who could not wait for the religious festival to be over so that he could get back to buying and selling. This person also made the ephah, with which he measured the grain, smaller than it should have been, and the shekel, with which he weighed the customers' money, bigger than it should have been. Dishonest business did not die out with

Amos; only the methods have changed. If we were expounding Amos 8 we should be morally bound to preach on this subject.

Guidelines in expounding the prophets

1. Find out all you can about the circumstances of the day, the way people lived, their human experiences, their fears and problems, their good and bad points

Then you can understand better the kind of message the prophet was bringing them from God. Many of the prophets lived in days of chaos and crisis very similar to our own, when governments were changing and society seemed to be falling apart and when the life of the ordinary people was very hard. Others were around when people were facing the challenge of prosperity.

Unfortunately the only way to find out about these circumstances is to read commentaries that explain them to us. While you can learn a certain amount from such passages as that quoted in Amos above, you can never get the full background of the prophets from their own writings. Even the reading of a good book on the history of Israel will help you to understand, for instance, why Jeremiah takes such a sad line and why Haggai talks about earning wages 'to put them into a bag with holes', a most fitting illustration of the problems of inflation.

Men do not really change over the years and you are preaching to a human condition. You therefore want to know just what the condition was then and to translate that experience into that of your hearers. To take Haggai again, the first few verses make it clear that some people had managed to build fairly luxurious houses since they had returned from exile in Babylon, because they had panelled walls. Yet at the same time they had 'planted much, but have harvested little. You eat, but never have enough. You drink, but never have your fill. You put on clothes, but are not warm.' Obviously the economy was not doing very well. This was the human condition that the prophet found and it is one that is very common in many countries today.

2. Know what God had to say to this human condition and the answers he was giving to the people

Haggai was told by God that the reason their harvests were not very good was because the Lord deliberately frustrated their hopes and when they had gathered in their little harvest he 'blew it away'. In other words, this was an act of judgement on God's part. The reason for this act of judgement was that the people had completely neglected the building of the house of God. They had panelled houses for themselves, but God's house 'remains a ruin'. They had their priorities wrong. They were professing believers, but were living as materialists, refusing to put God first. You do not need to look very far to see a clear application to many of our circumstances today. We use different coins or pieces of paper to count our money and we may not need to build a magnificent house for God, but the principle of self first, or material things before God, is just the same.

3. Pay great attention to the main verbs

This may sound an obvious piece of advice that is quite elementary from the viewpoint of grammar, but it is amazing how little it is practised.

4. Pay great attention to the symbolism of the prophets

This is a very common feature in the prophets which does not appear so often in other passages of Scripture. Here a good imagination is a great help, not to invent, but to see into a symbol. Ezekiel was told that his ministry would be opposed and be uncomfortable. The Lord said, 'Though briars and thorns are all around you and you live among scorpions . . .' No one who has ever walked through the jungle needs too much imagination to know what the Lord meant by briars and thorns being all around and no one who has been bitten by a scorpion will want to live among them! Ezekiel and John were both told to eat books. What better picture could there be for reading, marking, learning and inwardly digesting a book and making it part of yourself? Jeremiah was sent to the pottery to see a vessel that was spoilt in the hand of the potter and to learn that God can take spoilt human clay and make another vessel out of it.

Sometimes, of course, the prophets do look into the

future, and there we must be very careful in defining what is intended as symbol and what is intended as fact. Commentators are divided, for instance, over the question whether the temple that Ezekiel sees towards the end of his book is ever going to be built. Some feel that it is symbolic of the ideal community and point to the picture of the new Jerusalem in Revelation. Others feel that this temple will in fact be built in Israel one day. Obviously each man has to be persuaded in his own mind, but I suggest that in our preaching we should hesitate to be dogmatic on such points. Jehovah's Witnesses have gone astray on a point of symbolism by taking the 144,000 who are sealed in Revelation 7 as being a literal number. Much of the symbolism of the prophets, however, is simply picture language to bring home a point forcibly.

Practical application

Let us now look at a passage from Hosea and treat it in the same way as previously, writing out the passage to help our understanding (see Table VI). The passage is chapter 14:1–9 and is part of a book addressed to the northern kingdom of Israel, who had been enjoying a period of great prosperity, but who morally and religiously had gone far astray. Their sins had been portrayed very clearly and God's love had been shown by an acted parable in which Hosea himself married a woman of loose morals and even bought her back from the slave market as a picture of the love of God for his people.

An interpretation

This passage is clearly one about the nature and fruits of true repentance. A people who had rejected their God and gone right away from him were invited to return and promised wonderful blessings if they did so. I would therefore preach on such a passage in accordance with an outline like the one below. Before I set that out, please notice the symbolism that runs right through the whole passage. Not only is it

---

Table VI. Analysis of Hosea 14:1—9

v. 1 Return, O Israel,	An invitation to repent.
to the Lord your God.	Come back to the Lord.
Your sins have been	Sins cause falling and
your downfall!	failure.
v. 2 Take words with you and	Open confession needed,
return to the Lord.	turning round to face the Lord.
Say to him: 'Forgive all our	Asking for general
sins and	forgiveness,
receive us	depending upon his
graciously,	gracious love.
that we may offer	The promise of new
the fruit of our	dedication.
lips.	
v. 3 Assyria cannot save us;	Renouncing of specific sins— no reliance on politics,
we will not mount	nor reliance on
war-horses.	military might,
We will never again say	no reliance on
'Our gods'	idolatry,
to what our own	on self-made
hands have made,	gods.
for in you the fatherless	Renewed trust in God.
find compassion.'	
v. 4 'I will heal their waywardness	God's response in grace . . . healing
and love them freely,	as Hosea loved his wayward wife.
for my anger has turned	Wrath real but removed.
away from them.	
v. 5 I will be like the dew to Israel;	Vital supply in a dry land.
he will blossom like a lily.	Pure beauty.
Like a cedar of Lebanon	Symbol of strength.
he will send down	Rooted in God.
his roots;	
v. 6 his young shoots will	Renewal of life.
grow.	
His splendour will be like	Refreshment.
an olive tree,	
his fragrance like a cedar	Attractiveness.
of Lebanon.	

Table VI (cont'd).

v. 7	Men will dwell again in his shade.	Helpfulness to others.
	He will flourish like the grain.	A harvest of righteousness.
	He will blossom like a vine,	Fruitfulness.
	and his fame will be like the wine from Lebanon.	Others soon know when God's people are restored.
v. 8	O Ephraim, what more have I to do with idols?	The repentant heart.
	I will answer him and care for him.	The responsive Lord.
	I am like a green pine tree;	The flourishing believer.
	your fruitfulness comes from me.'	The source of his flourishing
v. 9	Who is wise? He will realize these things.	We must learn from others' mistakes.
	Who is discerning? He will understand them.	We must learn to discern:
	The ways of the Lord are right;	1. God is always right.
	the righteous walk in them,	2. To be right with God is right.
	but the rebellious stumble in them.	3. Rebellion against God and departure from his ways only hurts ourselves.

there in such obvious parallels as the beauty of the lily, but also in a sentence like: 'Assyria cannot save us.' One of Israel's frequent sins was trusting in political scheming instead of in the power of God and it led her into continual trouble with her neighbours. Likewise, the reference to riding on horses was a clear reference to military power, for the horse was the most important item of military equipment.

Sermon outline

Subject: The need and the promise of revival

1. *The invitation to repent*
God invites Israel, as he invites us, to return to him in repentance. There can be no revival without repentance.

This passage enables us to understand what true repentance is about.

The passage tells us that true repentance involves
Returning to the Lord whom we have forsaken (v. 1);
Acknowledging to the Lord that the cause of our troubles is our sin (v. 2);
Confessing with words and in detail what we have done or not done (v. 2).

Israel asked God to forgive her sins in general and to forgive . . .
reliance on political scheming instead of trusting God (v. 3);
reliance upon military resources (v. 3);
reliance upon self-made gods and answers (v. 3).
In our case the corresponding sins could well be
reliance upon our own plans and schemes to solve problems;
reliance upon powerful people to use their influence;
trusting in some man-made scheme — in, for example, fund-raising.
Israel finally confessed that only in the Lord could she find true compassion (v. 3).

Since the garden of Eden, man has tried to find answers to his needs on his own and independently of God.

Such answers are no answers at all and we have to come to God and confess this.

2. *The promise to restore*
When God's people do in fact return to him in this way, then he makes promises to them. He promises:
to bring healing of their waywardness (v. 4);
to pour out his love on them freely (v. 4).
(Here the example of Hosea can be introduced.)
to refresh and renew his people, as the dew brought new life to the dry fields of Israel in the hot season (v. 5).

The result of this unseen, yet real healing, love and renewing will be seen in

damaged lives restored — to beauty (v. 5);
                          — to strength (v. 5);
                          — to growth (v. 6);
                          — to fruitfulness (v. 6);
                          — to attractiveness (v. 6).

Under God's care and cultivation, his people will again become fruitful and be helpful to others.

3. The advice to take notice

Scripture was written so that we might learn from it.
True wisdom lies in taking note of its lessons (v. 9).
We need to realize that they are for us to understand.
So we can learn three lessons from Israel's sin and her repentance:

1. The ways of the Lord are right and therefore common sense calls for our following them and not our own paths (v. 9).
2. Righteousness is walking in the right paths that God has laid down for us.
3. If we wish to be rebellious we must expect problems.
   We fall over our own schemes and stumble through life (v. 9).

Once again these notes are just the bare bones of what I would normally have written down, but I have set them down here to illustrate how the writing out of the passage can help in the preparation of a message that comes straight from the Word of God itself. The prophets are the most wonderful writings, but they are also very much neglected in the church today.

Study questions

1. Analyse Ezekiel 2:8—3:11 and outline a message on the responsibilities and privilege of the minister of the Word of God.
2. What is the meaning of the symbols in Isaiah 40:1—11; Daniel 7:19—22 and the following symbols in Amos:

cows of Bashan (4:1), justice and righteousness compared to a river and never-failing stream (5:24) and the horses who run on rocky crags, and the oxen that plough there (6:12)?

3. Write down modern equivalents for the symbols expressed in Amos in 2 above. Use terms that would be meaningful to city-dwellers.

10.
The introduction

Definition

The introduction to a sermon is the means by which the thoughts of the hearers are brought into line with the thoughts of the speaker in the shortest possible time. When you stand up to speak, the mind of each hearer is filled with all kinds of thoughts, ranging from wondering if she has enough food for the next meal to worrying how he is going to repay some debt. However, people do not know what you are going to speak about and are therefore curious for a moment to find out. This is your opportunity to gain entrance, to fasten on that moment of curiosity and to lead your hearers to think what you want them to think. Gain their attention now, and you may keep them for the whole message, lose their attention now, and you will probably never get it back again. Attentive faces are no guarantee of attentive minds. Children let us know when they are bored because they fidget and look all over the place, but adults have learnt to hide their feelings and to look interested when in fact their thoughts are thousands of miles away. Nor can you assume that all of your hearers want to be led in the direction of your thoughts. Some of them no doubt are anxious to hear the Word of God, but others are only casually interested and others not at all. You have to lead them from what concerns them now to what you want them to think about, and that may be something that has never before concerned them.

It is at this point that the earlier part of the service is so important. If people's minds have been moved by the worship to turn their thoughts towards God, they are much more likely to hear what his Word has to say. True worship

not only glorifies God, but prepares men to hear his truth.
I have preached in churches where I felt as though I hardly
needed to say anything at all. God was so obviously present
with us that when I stood up to speak I felt that half of
my work had already been done for me. I have also preached
in churches where the first half of the message has been
spent in a tough battle to gain entrance into the minds of
the congregation, who were obviously completely unprepared
by the worship to listen to the Word of God and quite
unused to giving their minds to the sermon.

Thorough preparation is a must

A good introduction is therefore one of the key parts of a
sermon and the preparation given to it may mean the difference between success and failure in communication. A good
introduction will be relevant both to the hearers' circumstances and to the theme of the sermon. You may be thrilled
with the theme of your sermon, but as yet no one else is;
so you have to begin where people are and move them on
from there. Again, you may be wonderfully relevant to the
circumstances of the hearers, but if you do not link them
up with your theme, you will lose them immediately your
introduction is over. A bridge has to have foundations on
both sides of the gap. If you begin by saying, 'The church
in Philippi was founded on Paul's second missionary journey
in A.D. 53 . . .', some people will not be listening by the
time you get to your second sentence. A.D. 53 to them is
so far in the past that you have already made clear to them
that what you have to say has nothing to do with their
everyday lives. Similarly, to begin by stating the obvious
is to invite inattention. 'Today is Christmas Day,' neither
informs nor inspires. Nor does it help if you use long words
to state the obvious. I once heard a famous speaker begin
by saying, 'We all live in a thoroughly contemporary
situation.' That sounds very learned, but when you put it
in plain and simple terms it really means: 'We are all alive
now!' Sometimes you may be tempted to make use of a
story you have heard, that has impressed you as a good
story, that would certainly get people's attention. But if

the story has nothing to do with the theme of your message for that day you are wasting your time, for you still have to build your bridge at the other side of the gap and valuable time has been used to no purpose. In fact a good introduction is more than a bridge, for a bridge can be used or not at the user's wish, but a good introduction compels your hearers to come with you in spite of themselves. It plays the role of a baited hook in fishing.

Characteristics of a good introduction

1. Arrests attention
Television advertisers are expert at this. They only have thirty seconds in which to get their point across and they do it effectively. Market sellers are also experts in drawing attention to their stalls, whether through special offers or an endless stream of talk geared to gaining your attention. They know that unless they gain your attention they will not sell anything. If you never look at the stall, how can you buy its wares? We need to be just as sceptical about some of our hearers' interest in listening to us and we have the most wonderful good news to share with them.

2. Moves from the known to the unknown
The more unknown the topic of your message, the harder you will have to work to bring your congregation with you. Some messages need little introduction because their theme lies close to the experience of the people, but others need much more careful introduction, either because of the difficulty of the subject, or the lack of experience of the hearers. Whatever the circumstances, the introduction must be seen to move from the known to the unknown.

3. Introduces the message briefly and clearly
Some introductions are almost another sermon in themselves, or the preacher gets so carried away with a wonderful story and all its details that when he eventually reaches his message it is rather an anticlimax and the congregation falls back into sleepiness. Introductions are meant to introduce and not to draw attention to themselves.

4. Presents a varied approach to the message

Do not always begin with a story. Do not always begin with a proverb. Do not always begin with a dramatic situation. Once a congregation feels that the preacher has a favourite way of introducing his message, they will know what to expect and the important sense of curiosity will be lacking.

5. Serves the theme of the message

Introductions should not be so dramatic that the rest of the message is dull by comparison. They must be very carefully prepared and thought out, and because they are to serve the main theme they should usually be prepared last of all. How can you prepare an introduction to a message if you are not sure exactly what that message will have as its main thrust?

6. Introduces a justifiable and valid message

To lead people to expect that you are going to answer the whole problem of pain in one sermon is to ask for people to go away disappointed. Pure honesty requires that the Christian does not claim more for his message than he intends to put into it, so, in trying to catch attention with your introduction, you must be careful not to carry things too far and claim for what you are about to say more than is justified.

7. Prepares people to hear the voice of the Spirit of God

A good introduction sets the tone of the message as well as introducing its contents. I am not suggesting that you set out to create an artificial emotional atmosphere, but that your opening sentences and the attitude that goes with them can set the right tone for what you wish to say. The Spirit of God himself must move in people's hearts, but a good introduction from a heart under the control of the Spirit is very significant.

Types of sermon introduction

Let us now consider different ways in which a sermon can be introduced.

1. Illustrations

Use an illustration that is familiar to the hearer's experience
and apply it to the topic in hand. Jesus began to speak to
the fishermen who had just caught a most wonderful haul
of fish by saying to them, 'Follow me, and I will make
you fishers of men.' There was enough of the familiar in
this to make such a saying perfectly easy to understand,
but also enough of the unknown to make the disciples
want to know more. How could they become fishers of
men, and what did fishing for men mean in any case? So
Jesus used a simple sentence to fasten the disciples' attention
upon him. Paul, when preaching in Athens, took hold of
the current religious situation. He said, 'Men of Athens!
I see that in every way you are very religious . . .' (Acts
17:22). He complimented his hearers on their attention
to the matter of knowing God and then pointed out that
he had come to tell them about the 'unknown God' to
whom they had built an altar. The King James Version
does not give the right sense to modern ears here, when
Paul is quoted as saying that the Athenians were 'very super-
stitious'. You do not attract the attention of the hearers
in the right way by suggesting that they are very super-
stitious, but that was not what Paul meant. He took a known
fact about Athenian life and used it to introduce the gospel
and to introduce it in the context of their own culture.

2. Striking statement

A sermon can be introduced by a statement that causes
surprise. Jesus said in Mark 2:5, 'Son, your sins are for-
given . . .' Immediately the whole house full of people
wanted an explanation; all were on their toes to hear and
see what would come next. This was an outrageous statement and demanded an explanation. Obviously this kind
of introduction has to be handled with care lest it be so
surprising that it raises hopes that cannot be justified or
proves to be untrue.

You may say something that will make people curious.
Jesus used this method with the woman of Samaria: 'If
you knew the gift of God, and who it is that asks you for a
drink, you would have asked him and he would have given
you living water' (John 4:10). Being human she could not

wait to find out exactly what the gift was and who Jesus was, and that is exactly what Jesus wanted to tell her! If you can only make people eager and anxious to hear what you are wanting to tell them, your battle is won. Children, of course, respond magnificently to this kind of introduction. A closed box, a covered jar, or simply a closed fist can have them on the edge of their seats wanting to know exactly what is inside and, if the truth is told, their parents are just as interested.

3. Proverb
Most languages have plenty of proverbs or pithy sayings. Where the listeners know these proverbs and where they form an important part of a culture, they can be used with great effect to gain interest. Jesus often quoted contemporary proverbs, not only in introductions, but at other times too. Part of Jeremiah's introduction to the glories of the new covenant in Jeremiah 31:29, 30 took a common saying that 'The fathers have eaten sour grapes, and the children's teeth are set on edge,' as a jumping-off ground for introducing personal responsibility and the grace of God to sinners in the coming new age.

4. Questions
Even a question can be used for the introduction, provided that it really creates interest. In Mark 2:19 Jesus began a short message on the need for all things to be new by the question: 'How can the guests of the bridegroom fast while he is with them?' The masterly way in which the Lord used the ordinary facts of everyday life to introduce his messages, short or long, is a lesson to all preachers. Long and involved questions are obviously not to be used: 'What in your opinion should be the supreme objective of the life of the Christian, to the attainment of which he should aim?' Such a question would deter the keenest listener.

5. A story
Here you have to be careful that the story is brief and relevant to the theme. Avoid anything that takes away from the main message. Some preachers are good at telling stories and are tempted to make more of the story than

the truth it is meant to illustrate. Jesus was, of course, the
master storyteller, but he never wasted words and always
went to the heart of the problem.

6. Dramatic action

Dramatic action has similarities to words spoken to make
people curious. It forces itself on their attention. This
method of introducing a sermon has to be used quite
sparingly, for the pulpit is no stage, but very occasionally
to do something that wakes the sleepiest member of the
congregation with a jolt serves to gain attention.

Jesus did it in the synagogue in his home town of Nazareth
simply by sitting down. He had come to his home town
after the start of his ministry and his reputation was spread-
ing around. When he stood up to read, as any member was
entitled to do, people were naturally curious to know what
would happen. When, however, he handed back the scroll
and sat down you could have cut the atmosphere with a
knife. By simply sitting down he was claiming the right to
preach, and the whole assembly was bursting to know what
this local young man, of whom they had heard so much,
was going to say. The action though simple was dramatic
and effective.

The story is told of a student who stopped in a London
street and pointed up to the top of a tall building where
a gospel text was standing out. Soon a crowd of people
gathered round to look at the place to which he was point-
ing. Then, when they had looked at the poster he quietly
walked away and left them.

Dramatic action can also be matched by a careful and
heartfelt reading of the text. Some passages of the Bible
are intensely dramatic. Used with care and with careful
use of pauses as well as speaking, such passages grip your
congregation at once. John 13:30 is a case in point. You
could begin a message something like this: '. . . "And it
was night." Yes, dark, impenetrable, irreversible night.
Night in the street. Night in Judas' soul. "He immediately
went out, and it was night." ' Spoken slowly and with feeling, this introduction never fails to grip.

Write your introduction

Because the introduction is such a vital part of the sermon, write out *the exact words you intend to use.* You do not have to feel absolutely bound by them, but those first words are vital to the success of the whole operation and if you are vague in your own mind how you are going to begin, then everyone else will be. If you have words clearly set out in front of you, then even if you begin in a completely unreceptive atmosphere you will have something meaningful to say in those first vital moments.

Above all things, in introducing your message avoid being apologetic. I remember a certain bishop in England who would usually begin any talk by saying, 'Of course, I really don't know why you people should be listening to someone like me.' From then on everyone took him at his word and stopped listening. Peter exhorts us, 'If any man speak, let him speak as the oracles of God.' The humility of the messenger is not meant to be a false one and you are, after all, the messenger of the Almighty. It is his Word you bring and that requires no apology.

Study questions

1. Prepare introductions to the messages on the widow's gift, on Hosea 14 and on Psalm 19 included in this book.
2. How were the following messages introduced: Peter's sermon on the Day of Pentecost (Acts 2); Jesus' message on the cost of discipleship (Mark 10:23–31); Paul's message to the hostile crowd (Acts 22)?
3. Note down the way five messages you hear are introduced and later ask yourself:
   a. Was the introduction effective in gaining your interest?
   b. What different ways were used?
   c. Were they too long or too short?
   d. Did they effectively link the experiences of the hearers with the message of the speaker?

11.
Illustrations

Chambers' Dictionary defines the verb 'to illustrate' as 'to make bright, to adorn . . . to make clear to the mind, to explain and adorn with pictures'. Sermon illustrations should do just these things. They should bring fresh light and brightness into the message, make the truth clearer to the mind and enable the hearer to picture in plain terms something that may be quite difficult to understand. They are not the message; they illustrate the message. You have to be careful in case your illustrations run away with you and become the main point of the sermon. People will very often remember good illustrations, but if they only remember those, and not the truth they were meant to illustrate, you will have failed.

Important pointers

When using an illustration check these important points:

1. Know what an illustration is meant to clarify!
If you forget it halfway through, your congregation are not going to receive more light. This, of course, means that you must be thoroughly familiar with the illustration, and not suddenly pick on it because you heard someone else tell a good story. Illustrations need as much preparation as any other part of the message, although that does not mean you should be afraid of introducing one that has just come into your mind if you are sure that it will really illustrate your point.

2. Use an illustration to highlight just one thing
If you use the one illustration to point to half a dozen

lessons, the chances are that your hearers will either be muddled or bored by the time you reach the end. Let me illustrate from the use of a slide transparency, which, after all, is a picture in the terms of the dictionary definition given above. A person who really knows how to use a slide will keep it on the screen for a very short time, just a few seconds. He will let the picture tell its own story and will not need to explain: 'I put this slide on to show you that tiny building in the back there behind all those people; you cannot see it very well, but that is where we live.' If he needs to do that he might as well have never shown the slide. Again, some people will keep the slide on for a very long time and describe for you every small detail all over the picture. This defeats the whole object of showing it in the first place. When Jesus spoke his parables he had one main object in view and he did not need to explain it for men to get the message.

3. Add the illustration to the message
Many times have I sat through enthralling messages by evangelists that went from story to story and had the audience listening to every word, only to find at the end of the message that sin, repentance and sometimes even the cross have scarcely been mentioned and the Scriptures hardly at all. The Word of God applied by the Spirit of God convicts men of sin and turns them to the Saviour. Your illustrations must serve the message, not rule it.

4. Fit your illustration to your audience
Sometimes Western preachers visit Asia or Africa and bring with them wonderful illustrations that in their own culture speak very clearly, but have no meaning for their listeners. If you are speaking to rural people, city illustrations bring little light. On one occasion a visiting missionary was picturing the disciples after the resurrection going out fishing again. She pictured the scene with the moon shining on the water. The trouble was that her hearers were fishermen, and they know that a good fisherman does not go fishing in the moonlight, because the fish are not around for catching then. If you are preaching to people you know well, there should be no problem, but if you are visiting

somewhere else it is useful to check your illustrations
beforehand.

5. Reduce your illustration to the essentials
In a sense this is the same as emphasizing one point, but it
also means cutting out anything in the story or parallel
situation that is not strictly relevant to the point you want
to make. Once again, a good slide transparency is neither
too dark nor too light, and the object you want people
to see is clearly the centre of attraction as soon as the slide
appears on the screen.

6. Use more illustrations for less interested audiences
This may mean that they are not so well instructed in the
faith, or it may mean that their culture is such that they are
not used to listening to connected discourses. A man who
works in the fields all day is probably very tired by the
evening, and his mind does not commonly think in abstract
terms. Truth therefore must be made to live before his
eyes so that he is drawn to it and can picture it in concrete
terms.

7. Beware of relying on illustrations too much
Otherwise there is a danger that, as with the evangelist
above, the illustration may crowd out the message. From
this angle too you need to beware of the use of humour in
messages. A touch of humour can bring home a point very
clearly, but you must be able to bring the people back to
the point and sometimes too much humour makes that
impossible. While you want to communicate as clearly
and effectively as possible, never forget that spiritual
effectiveness comes from a living touch with Christ, not
from ability to tell good stories.

Source of illustrations

1. The Bible
The Bible itself is one of the best places in which to find
illustrations. God's revelation has always been clothed in
actions as well as in words to explain those actions. The

redemption of Israel from Egypt is in one sense one long and glorious illustration of man's deliverance from the bondage of sin. God has acted out his message to man in human history, and the Old Testament is a fund of illustrations of New Testament truth. Unfortunately many people do not know their Old Testament, but by using some of the stories from it as illustrations of New Testament doctrines you can make truth clear and show the relevance of the Old Testament at the same time.

Several of the prophets expressed their message in terms of apt illustrations. Jeremiah, for instance, was told to take a girdle or belt that was brand-new and to wear it. Then he was sent to the river Euphrates to hide it in a cleft of a rock. After some time he went back to recover the belt and found that it was useless. The whole action was God's way of illustrating the judgement that was coming on his people Israel through their exile (Jer. 13:1–7).

In Amos 3:3–8, the prophet wanted to show that he was speaking his unwelcome message to Israel only because God had told him to do so. So he used a series of illustrations, all of which made it plain that nothing happens without a valid cause. People do not walk together unless they have agreed to do so; a lion does not roar unless he has some prey; a bird does not suddenly fall to the ground unless it has been caught in a snare; and when the war trumpet sounds, people tremble. Even so, said Amos, when God speaks the prophet has to say something.

Stephen's speech in Acts 7 also shows an effective use of biblical illustrations. We probably find this passage quite difficult to understand. So much of it seems to be a pointless recital of Israel's history. To his hearers, however, Stephen's intention was very clear, for he chose passages of their history to show how often Israel had been unwilling to move forward with God and how often they had refused to accept their deliverers. In just the same way, they were refusing to accept the Saviour from heaven. Stephen's illustrations were so clear that in the end his hearers wanted to stone him.

In 1 Corinthians 10:11 we read, 'These things happened to them as examples, and they were written down as warnings for us . . .' In other words, the Old Testament is the ideal source of illustrations for the Christian preacher.

2. History
History provides another source of illustrations. However, this is one that has to be used with care, especially in a cross-cultural context. We are all familiar with our own history, but other people may never have heard of our heroes or understand why they were important.

3. Topical events
Even in remote areas, the transistor radio abounds these days so that everyone knows what are the main items of news. In the city areas there is good value to be gained from reading the newspaper, for an illustration of something that only happened yesterday comes home with great force.

4. Everyday events in the life of the community
A pastoral visitation will tell many things that will illustrate the truth of different Scriptures, though, of course, the preacher must be careful not to be too personal in his speaking.

Life is so full of variety and the same human problems come again and again in so many different ways that illustrations should not normally be difficult to find when needed. They may occur to you in the course of writing out your sermon, or you may wish to go through the written material afterwards to decide where an illustration could best be used and which one it should be, but let them fit naturally and not be forced.

Illustrations have limitations

One final piece of advice is to remember that the best of illustrations have their limitations. None of them is complete. At best they serve to illustrate, to shed some light. They are not foolproof. When thinking, for instance, of the Trinity, there is no illustration existing that can possibly light up all the truth, for the truth of God in his innermost being is beyond human analysis anyway. Yet an illustration may serve to make more understandable that which is deeper than all human reason. We might take the illustration of the sun, for instance. When we look at the sun we do not actually see the sun, but the brightness of the sun. If we looked upon the sun itself we should be blinded. In the same way, we cannot see God, though he is real, but in the Bible we can see him who is the radiance of God's glory and the exact representation of his being, Jesus Christ, the brightness of his Father's glory. Yet at the same time we speak of feeling the sun on our bodies. What we feel is neither the sun itself, nor the brightness of the sun, but the warmth of the rays of the sun, which are invisible. In the same way the Holy Spirit, who is invisible, is yet real to our hearts and by his presence we are made aware of God. Yet the sun that is there and whose brightness we see and whose rays we feel is one sun, not three. Now I have found this illustration very helpful in shedding light on the doctrine of the Trinity, even though there are many ways in which the illustration breaks down, for there are many kinds of analogy with the sun which are not true of the Trinity, quite apart from the fact that the sun is not personal in the first place. The illustration is not foolproof, but used properly it does shed light, it does illustrate.

Study questions

1. Prepare an illustration to show:
   a. that unseen things are not necessarily unreal;
   b. the meaning of faith in God;
   c. the power of love in human relationships;
   d. the folly of concentrating only on material things.
2. Why do you think Stephen talked about Joseph (Acts 7:9—16), Moses (vv. 35—41) and the tabernacle and temple (vv. 44—47) when defending himself before the Sanhedrin?
3. In preaching on Ephesians 1:1—10 how would you illustrate the following: God's love to us before the world began; the free gift we receive as compared with the cost he paid; the riches of his grace lavished upon us?

12.
The conclusion

Appeal to the whole man

When God speaks to man he speaks to the whole man and the preaching of the Word of God should address itself to the whole man, too. When Peter preached the first Christian sermon on the Day of Pentecost he was careful to speak to the *mind*, the *heart* and the *will*.

Address to the mind

His message was based on clear reasoning. He pointed out that the disciples could not possibly be drunk because it was too early in the day. On the contrary, what the people had seen happening before their eyes was a fulfilment of the Word of God in the prophet Joel. Peter then developed a closely reasoned argument that Jesus of Nazareth was risen from the dead and the apostles were witnesses to that and so were the Scriptures. This Jesus, being clearly raised from the dead, had received the gift of the Holy Spirit from the Father and sent him forth upon his people. Therefore the existence of what the people could see that day was in itself proof that this same Jesus was both Lord of all and the promised Messiah. This was an argument addressed to the mind, and it needed careful following. Our preaching must also be addressed to the minds of men, so that they understand the real basis of that which we preach.

Address to the emotions

But Peter did not stop there. His sermon struck at the emotions, at the heart of the people. This Jesus, whom God had so clearly made both Lord and Christ, was the very same Jesus that those same people had crucified. They were morally responsible for the death of the Messiah and the crucifixion and rejection of the Son of God. This was the climax of Peter's sermon and the effect on his hearers was that they were cut to the heart. Peter was not afraid to move the emotions of men, nor should we be. The moving was based upon truth presented to the mind, but the moving was none the less real. Preaching that never moves the emotions has something wrong with it.

Address to the will
Yet Peter did not end there. In fact the people gave him no choice, for they asked him right away, 'Brethren, what shall we do?' Until the will of man has been moved to do something about what he has understood with his mind and felt in his heart, the work of God is incomplete. Peter then applied his message by urging the people to repent and be baptized in the name of Jesus Christ; they would then receive both the forgiveness of their sins and the gift of the Holy Spirit.

Preaching that simply informs the mind leads to intellectualism. Preaching that only moves the heart leads to emotionalism, and preaching that only affects the will leads to Pharisaism. Reason, feeling, will – all three elements must be present in your preaching if it is to be truly biblical. In a sense all three elements must be present throughout your preaching, so that the truth is applied as it is expounded, and yet the concluding part of the sermon is vitally important in gathering together all that has been said so that the mind is clear, the heart warm and the will active to translate God's Word into life. Paul's practice in ministry he described to the Ephesian elders in Acts 20:20, 21 as *preaching* what was helpful, *teaching* publicly and from house to house, and *declaring* the need of turning to God in repentance and of faith in our Lord Jesus Christ. The *preaching* means an announcing, the declaring of the facts of the gospel; the *teaching* involves explanation of all that those facts involved and the *declaring* is exhortation to do something about it in terms of the response of repentance and faith. His ministry would not have been complete without expecting action on the part of his hearers.

Characteristics of an effective conclusion

1. Comprehensive and emphatic

There should be a summary of the teaching of the whole passage, so that everything is seen as a whole and not only summarized but emphasized. The points you have made should be gathered together so that people are reminded of them and see how they link with each other and lead to the conclusion you have stated. Repetition is one of the important parts of good teaching, and if you present your main points over again people are reminded of them and they should be able to go away remembering them. However, it is important that this summary should be a summary and not a repetition of the whole message. That would be tedious and should be unnecessary.

2. Clear and relevant

There should be clear application of the truth proclaimed in terms of the lives of the listeners. The moral and spiritual demands of the truth should be clear, relevant and pressed home, so that no one is in doubt where he/she stands or what is required of him/her. The power of the Holy Spirit was so manifest in Peter's sermon on the Day of Pentecost that the people interrupted him as he reached his climax and asked what they must do. Such things have happened again and again in history in times of revival. On other occasions, the application came as an integral part of the message. If you read Acts 3:16—26 and Acts 13:37—40 you will notice that not only did the apostles offer the benefits of the gospel, but they also warned against rejecting the truth. 'Anyone who does not listen to him will be completely cut off from among his people,' Peter boldly declared to the people in the temple (Acts 3:23). Truth not only carries blessing with acceptance, but loss with rejection. Paul likewise said in Pisidian Antioch, 'Take care that what the prophets have said does not happen to you: "Look, you scoffers, wonder and perish . . ." ' (Acts 13:40, 41).

3. Short and timely

The conclusion has often been spoilt because the preacher has not quite known how to finish. Because it is important to leave the hearers with the full impact of the message ringing in their ears, it is essential that you keep your conclusion short and not only *know how* to finish but *do* it. Preachers have been divided into two classes, in this respect: those who say 'lastly' and last, and those who say 'finally' and finish. The second kind are much to be preferred. This means that the conclusion needs at least as careful preparation as any other part of the address, and particularly that you know exactly how you will finish. This does not mean that under the guidance of the Holy Spirit you need to be bound to what you have written down and dare not change it, but it does mean that if you are not quite sure how to finish there is a last clear sentence written down in front of you to be used. Otherwise it is very easy to ramble on, because as you listen to yourself, each successive sentence does not seem quite the right one with which to end.

Study questions

1. In Acts 17:22–31 Paul preached to the Athenians. How did he approach their minds, their hearts and their wills? In which order did he tackle them and how much time in relation to the whole was spent on each? What results followed? What can we learn from this?
2. Write a conclusion to a message on Psalm 19 and to one on Hosea 14. If people asked you at the end of the message the question they asked Peter, 'Brothers, what shall we do?' how would you answer them?
3. Examine Jesus' conclusion to the Sermon on the Mount in Matthew 7:24–27. How did he make sure the message would not be lost? What impression did he leave with his hearers in verses 28, 29?

13.
The primary need

Presence and power of the Holy Spirit

'Our gospel came to you not simply with words, but also with power, with the Holy Spirit and with deep conviction' (1 Thess. 1:5). Paul, in writing to the Thessalonians, made no idle boast. The Thessalonian church was there to prove his claim. They knew what had happened and so did the whole district round about, for they not only believed his powerful word but preached it themselves all around the province.

Unless our preaching is visited with power and with the Holy Spirit and with much conviction, we are wasting our time. Simply adding another few thousand words to the overloaded air waves does not justify our existence. We are placed in our position as preachers to see lives changed.

Dr Martin Lloyd-Jones in his excellent book *Preaching and Preachers* distinguishes between the preparation of the sermon and the preaching of it. He points out that both of these activities are essential to success in the right sense. We cannot expect the Holy Spirit to honour our laziness if we prepare poorly. We must make every effort to see that we have learnt all we can from the message ourselves and have thought through how we will present it. Most of this present book is concerned with that preparation.

Yet the act of preaching is just as important as the preparation, and for this we need continual dependence on the presence and power of the Holy Spirit. Not that we can afford to prepare without this presence either, for he is the one to guide us into all truth and these things are spiritually discerned. Indeed our whole business as preachers, as far as our ministry to the church of God is concerned, can be summed up as follows: 'Not in words taught us by human wisdom but in words taught by the Spirit, expressing spiritual truth in spiritual words' (1 Cor. 2:13).

Self-evaluation and prayer

We must not lose sight of the great importance of the actual delivery of the message. If you preach regularly you will no doubt be familiar with the horrible feeling that hits you when a sermon has fallen quite flat. Perhaps you spent hours in preparing that message and maybe it thrilled your soul right through at that time, but when it came to the preaching you might as well have been talking about the price of fish to a brick wall. Not that we are always the best judge of the effectiveness of our own messages. You may have felt terrible and there may even have been physical reasons why you did, but that does not mean that God has not used your message to speak to some person when he or she needed it most. On the other hand, you can leave the pulpit feeling thrilled with your own message and having thoroughly enjoyed giving it, only to find that no one else enjoyed it at all. God has his own ways of keeping us humble, and this is one of them. Certainly, the period immediately after the delivery of a sermon is not the time realistically to assess your ministry. Praise at that moment can lead to pride and criticism to despair. So if someone is helping you to improve your presentation, do suggest to them that they make no comments for twenty-four hours. And for yourself, you are too emotionally involved to be able to make any true assessment, so the best thing to do is to commit the message to the Lord for his use and dismiss it from your mind. That, however, is not to suggest that you should not follow that message with prayer later in the day, but then the prayer is centred on the people and not on yourself.

Review for additional thoughts

Once the preparation of a sermon has been completed and

put in note form it can be left until near the time of delivery.
Then you need to go through it once again, maybe adding a
few fresh thoughts as they occur and warming to the theme
again yourself. This is absolutely essential. The best
preparation served cold is like a curry without the curry
powder. Paul exhorted Timothy to 'watch your life and
doctrine closely'. The first part of this word of advice is
as essential if not more so than the second. If preaching
is truth mediated through personality, that personality
needs to be under the control of the Holy Spirit.

Free time before preaching

Perhaps I may mention here how difficult we often make
it for our preachers by keeping them busy right up until
the last moment before the service. Perhaps the minister
is expected to be at the door of the church to welcome
people, but can no one else do that? More often, we are just
so busy that deacons or elders or wardens never have an
opportunity to spend a short time quietly with the minister
before the service, praying for the power of God to come
down. How can a man expect to go into the worship of
God with his heart fully prepared to deliver the message
of God to his people, if he has just had to sort out a tangle
in the choir or find a room for a Sunday School teacher
who has just arrived? The worship service may help him calm
down and gather his thoughts, but that is not what the
worship is for. If we want preaching with power in our
services we must free the preacher to prepare himself.

Dependence on the Holy Spirit

Preaching, then, demands constant dependence on the
Holy Spirit, firstly to illuminate your mind to the truth
of God, and secondly to empower your own spirit in the
time immediately before delivery, but also thirdly during
the actual period of speaking. Not that you are meant to
be self-conscious as you preach, but rather God-conscious
in constant dependence on his power. You cannot open

the hearts of men, or convict the sinner. You cannot warm the hearts of the cold, or revive the fallen from their deadness. But God, in his mercy and grace, has wonderfully ordained that, through the foolishness of preaching, men should believe. You never know what he may accomplish, if you are dependent upon him. Paul described the Corinthian Christians as 'a letter from Christ delivered by us, written not with ink, but with the Spirit of the living God, not on tablets of stone but on tablets of human hearts'. The writer is Christ. The one who makes the mark on the heart is the Holy Spirit. But the preacher delivers the letter that makes all the difference for time and eternity. Part of the thrill of preaching is never knowing what God is going to do that day. Dependence on the Holy Spirit is not only necessary, it is completely rewarding.

A sermon worth repeating?

What about preaching a sermon more than once? Opinions differ widely, but most preachers have little choice but to repeat themselves and someone has said that if it is not worth repeating it is probably not worth preaching once. Yet you must be careful here. You probably have had the experience of preaching a sermon in the morning that proved to be powerful in the hands of God, and then repeating the same message in the evening and expecting the same result, only to be bitterly disappointed. I doubt whether it is ever wise to preach the same message twice in the same day, because if you have really given yourself on the first occasion you have not had sufficient time to recoup that strength for a second journey through the same countryside on the same day. It is rather like an Olympic runner in one of the long races who wins his heat in style only to find that his performance in the final is poor. He gave everything first time.

To change the metaphor to one used by the Rev. Alan Stibbs, a man of God much used in exposition, every fresh print from a negative in photography needs to be given more light. You need time to give that fresh light from the Holy Spirit on the old negative of your sermon notes. Never

assume that the second time will be easy, or that no preparation will be needed at all. That is a recipe for disaster. But
if you do prepare again and allow the Holy Spirit to rekindle
the fire in your heart, then the second, third, or tenth time
may well be more effective than the first.

Serious responsibility

Effectiveness in bringing the knowledge of God to men is
our aim. We thought at the very beginning of this book of
Hosea's judgement that the people's lack of knowledge went
right back to the priests' lack of instruction. Those given
the responsibility of teaching God's people must expect to
be held answerable for their people's ignorance. Who is
sufficient for these things?

Ezekiel also underlines the failure of the preachers of
his day to have any effect on the moral, religious and social
decline of the southern kingdom of Judah. They did plenty
of preaching and they used the right terms to describe it.
They said, 'Hear the Word of the Lord!' They spoke and
claimed the authority of God for their message, but he
refused to honour it. God sent Ezekiel to condemn them,
for they were those 'who prophesy out of their own
imagination'. They followed their own spirit and had seen
nothing! Their visions were false and their divinations a lie.
'The Lord has not sent them; yet they expect their words
to be fulfilled.' As a result they were described as 'jackals
among ruins', quite unaware of the devastation around
them and knocking pieces off the walls instead of getting
down to a repair job (see Ezek. 13:1—7). So is every preacher
who gets his message out of his own mind without dependence upon the Lord who called him, and who simply says
what he thinks his people need or want to hear. How can
we avoid such a terrible danger? By exposition.

Proclamation of God's unchanging Word

When we go back to the Word of God we find what he has
said, and indeed what he is always saying, for no word of

God is simply spoken and then left. God is still saying what
he has always said, whether it be the message of the judgement of God upon a generation like that of Ezekiel, or of
the love of God in Christ. Our job as servants of God and
of his Word is to translate the principles of his speaking
into terms that modern man can understand and obey.
Then we can truly say, 'Hear the Word of the Lord!' We
did not think it up. We might prefer not to have to say
what we find in front of us. Some of our congregation may
be offended, and we may find ourselves very unpopular
with them or with others who do not like what we say.
Yet in faithfulness to God and in a spirit of love we are
bound to proclaim the whole truth of God. Only then are
we faithful to our calling.

Study questions

1. What can we learn about preaching from 1 Corinthians 2? List the separate items and discuss them.
2. What can we learn about our ministry from Colossians
   4:2–6?
3. What reasons for confidence can we find in 2 Corinthians 3? On whom does the main ministry depend in
   this chapter?

Appendices

<u>Appendix A.</u> Analysis of Psalm 19

v. 1 The heavens declare the glory of God;
    the skies proclaim the work of his hands.
v. 2 Day after day they pour forth speech;
    night after night they display knowledge.
v. 3 There is no speech or language
      where their voice is not heard.
v. 4 Their voice goes out into all the earth,
    their words to the ends of the world
v. 5 in the heavens he has pitched a tent for the sun
        which is like a bridegroom coming forth
           from his pavilion,
        like a champion rejoicing to run his course.
v. 6   It rises at one end of the heavens
        and makes its circuit to the other;
        nothing is hid from its heat.

v. 7 The *law* of the Lord is *perfect, reviving* the soul.
    The *statutes* of the Lord are *trustworthy, making wise* the simple.
v. 8 The *precepts* of the Lord are *right, giving joy* to the heart.
    The *commands* of the Lord are *radiant, giving light* to the eyes.
v. 9 The *fear* of the Lord is *pure, enduring* for ever.
    The *ordinances* of the Lord are *sure* and altogether *righteous.*

v.10 They are more precious than gold, than much pure gold;
    they are sweeter than honey, than honey from the comb.
v.11 By them is your servant warned;
      in keeping them there is great reward.
v.12 Who can discern his errors?
    Forgive my hidden faults.
v.13 Keep your servant also from wilful sins;
    may they not rule over me.
        Then will I be blameless,
        innocent of great transgression.
v.14 May the words of my mouth and
        the meditation of my heart
        be pleasing in your sight,
    O Lord, my Rock and
      my Redeemer.

Creation only speaks of the *glory* of God.
What we have made tells something of who we are: so with God.
Continuous message given out.
Twenty-four hour communication.
Universal language; no barriers.
No one can 'jam' this broadcast.
No one is out of reach of this broadcast
(cf. Rom. 1:20, which leaves man without excuse for not believing).
The glory and finery of the sun in celebration
     limited to the course arranged, yet glorious;

     the joy of virile strength;
     universal appearance;

     universal feeling and experience.
The sun sums up the witness of the whole creation to the glory of
  God

Notice the pattern in the following verses:
the name for aspects of God's law;
the nature of his law;
the effect of his law when obeyed and implemented.
     God's message to men is
          perfect, trustworthy, right, radiant, pure and sure.
     It revives, makes wise, gives joy, gives light, goes on for ever
        and is absolutely right.
Therefore it is better than the most valuable thing.
It is sweeter than the sweetest thing.
The negative effect for positive benefit.
The positive effect for benefit.
Aware of errors.
The unconscious sins; the Word brings conviction.
Aware of weakness and need for prayer.
What begins with wilful sin ends in slavery to sin.
Freedom from accusation.
Big sins begin with little ones. Keep from them all.
     Prayer for the Lord to govern words and
        inmost thoughts.
     Where it really counts.
He is our strength and safety.
He restores us when we fail.

Appendix B. Preaching practice – evaluation form

Speaker   Date
Type of audience   Purpose
Subject or central theme

Main points:

Introduction:
Relevant   Brief   Arrests attention
Not exaggerated   Moves from known to unknown

Main exposition:
Arises clearly from the passage
Moves to a climax
Clear
Memorable
Compels attention to Scripture by hearers
Relevant to the needs of men

Illustrations:
Number
Clarity
Effectiveness of use
Relative to the audience

Conclusion:
Does it summarize and emphasize   Clarity
Application of truth to hearers   Brevity

General points:

Poise   Gestures   Habits
Looking at audience   Enthusiasm

Language:
Tone of voice   Volume   Audible

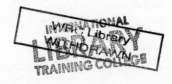